The SOUL *of* JESUS

The SOUL of JESUS
Contemplated in
Union with Mary

By Rev. E. Neubert, S.M., S.T.D.

Preface by The Most Rev. John Julian Weber
ARCHBISHOP OF STRASBOURG

Translated by Rev. Sylvester P. Juergens, S.M., S.T.D.

THE BRUCE PUBLISHING COMPANY • *Milwaukee*

NIHIL OBSTAT:

J. WILLIS LANGLINAIS, S.M., S.T.D.
Censor deputatus

IMPRIMI POTEST:

JAMES YOUNG, S.M.
Provincialis

NIHIL OBSTAT:

JOHN A. SCHULIEN, S.T.D.
Censor librorum

IMPRIMATUR:

✠ WILLIAM E. COUSINS
Archbishop of Milwaukee
October 1, 1962

This work is a translation of the French *L'âme de Jésus Contemplée Avec Marie,* published by Editions Alsatia, 17 Rue Cassette, Paris VIe, France.

ACKNOWLEDGMENT

I wish to thank Brother Julius Kreshel, S.M., lately deceased, and Sister Mary Concordia, C.S.J., for reading the translation and for helpful comments; also Brother Theodore Kauss, S.M., for preparing the manuscript for the printer, and Rev. John Dockter, S.M., and Brother Robert Janson, S.M., for reading the proofs.

THE TRANSLATOR

PREFACE

The French masters of the seventeenth century summarize Christian life in these words: to know, to love, and to imitate Christ. These three operations of the soul seem to them to sum up all that a disciple of Jesus has to do to become perfect.

In that view they are in complete accord with the teaching of the Apostles. "I count everything loss because of the excelling knowledge of Jesus Christ, my Lord. For his sake I have suffered the loss of all things." It is St. Paul who says that (Phil 3:8). The disciple of love adds: "He who says that he abides in him, ought himself also to walk just as he walked" (1 Jn 2:6). It would be easy to multiply citations in the same sense and to choose similar testimonies from the writings of the saints.

Who will teach us to know our Master profoundly, to love Him passionately, and to imitate Him faithfully? Will it not be especially His Mother, Mary? Nobody knew Him better than she: she brought Him forth into this world, wrapped Him in swaddling clothes, and laid Him in the manger; she lived intimately with Him many long years, watched Him during His journeys, and contemplated Him dying on the cross.

Who loved Him more dearly than she and showed that love by a more complete donation of herself? Would she be a mother without that love? Who shared His life more than she and collaborated more actively in His work of redemption? She is, therefore, eminently fit to help us realize that statement of Charles de Foucauld which sketches for us the road to perfection: "I have decided to maintain in me the will to work at transforming myself entirely into Jesus, with the aim of changing myself into another Jesus living and active, of transforming by Him and in Him all my thoughts, my words, my actions, my prayers, my sufferings, my whole life and my death" (*Spiritual Notes*).

This book has as its only purpose to help us make Christ our life (Phil 1:21) under the guidance and with the motherly assistance of her of whom "was born Jesus who is called Christ" (Mt 1:16). Its title is both attractive and unpretentious, THE SOUL OF JESUS CONTEMPLATED IN UNION WITH MARY. The author might have added as subtitle, "The Christian soul led by Mary to the love of Jesus, to the imitation of Him, in order to live in Him, and to live by Him completely in God and for God, in the service of His brothers." From this you see its great riches.

In his letter asking me to write this Preface, the author, well known for his work in Mariology, said: "This is not a work of exegesis but rather a book for spiritual reading and meditation. It aims at permitting the reader to learn better how 'to have this mind in you which was also in Christ Jesus' (Phil 2:5), under the direction of her who according to St. Pius X is the best teacher and guide to knowing Him." That is perfectly true. May I dare simply add that, if we have not here a book of exegesis, we do have an exposition that is based solidly and primarily on the Word of God, on the Gospels and the writings of the Apostles. That is the book's value and strength. It is up to the reader to judge for himself.

Feast of the Immaculate Heart of Mary
Strasbourg, August 22, 1957

JOHN JULIAN WEBER
Bishop of Strasbourg

CONTENTS

Preface vii

. . . INTRODUCTORY CHAPTERS
1 "I Have Given You An Example . . ." . . 1
2 Christ Our Life, According to St. Paul . . 5
3 Our Imitation of the Life of Christ, According
   to St. Paul 9
4 The Testimony of St. Teresa of the Child Jesus,
   The Little Flower 14
5 Testimony of the Masters of the Spiritual Life 19
6 With Mary to Contemplate Jesus . . . 25
7 The Holy Spirit Revealing Jesus . . . 30
8 Practical Advice 35

. . . THE SOUL OF JESUS
       CONSIDERED IN ITSELF
9 Reactions of the Body of Jesus Upon His Soul 42
10 The Intelligence of Jesus 48
11 The Will of Jesus 51
12 The Fears of Jesus 57
13 The Joys of Jesus 62
14 The Joys of Mary 66
15 Our Joys as Christians 70
16 The Sorrows of Jesus 74
17 The Sorrows of Mary 79
18 Our Sorrows 81

. . . THE SOUL OF JESUS AND
       THE FATHER
19 Jesus and the Father's Will 83
20 Mary and the Father's Will 88
21 Our Disposition Toward the Father's Will . 92

22 Jesus and the Glory of the Father . . . 95
23 Mary and the Glory of the Father . . . 99
24 The Father's Glory and Ourselves . . . 103
25 The Intimacy of Jesus with His Father . . 105
26 Mary's Childlike Intimacy with the Father . 109
27 Our Intimacy with the Heavenly Father . . 113

. . . THE SOUL OF JESUS AND MEN

28 The Mission of Jesus Among Men, A Mission
    of Love 116
29 Mary's Mission, One of Love 119
30 Our Mission, One of Love 121
31 Qualities of the Love of Jesus and Mary for
    Souls — And Ours 127

. . . THE SPECIAL LOVE OF JESUS FOR CERTAIN CLASSES OF PEOPLE

32 Love for the Poor 144
33 Love for the Afflicted 146
34 Love of Jesus for Sinners 152
35 Love of Jesus for the Pure of Heart . . . 160
36 The Love of Jesus for Generous Souls . . 162
37 Love of Jesus for His Apostles 164
38 Jesus and the Love for Enemies . . . 171

. . . WHAT JESUS REQUIRES OF US

39 The Simplicity of Evangelical Childhood . . 175
40 The Humility of Evangelical Childhood . . 179
41 Evangelical Confidence 182
42 Total Consecration and Total Renunciation . 186
43 Renouncing the World 190
44 My Yoke Is Sweet 193
45 Variety of Attitudes Among the Auditors of
    Jesus 197

The SOUL of JESUS

Chapter 1

"I HAVE GIVEN YOU AN EXAMPLE..."

At a particularly solemn moment of His life, on the point of instituting the Holy Eucharist together with the priesthood and of beginning His Passion, Jesus said to His disciples: "I have given you an example, that as I have done to you, so you also should do" (Jn 13:15). Previously He had told them, "When perfected, everyone will be like his teacher" (Lk 6:40).

Our great task, then, is to imitate Christ. It is not to observe always what is right in the Commandments of God and from time to time to remember Christ, for instance, on Sunday to assist at Mass, on Easter to receive His Body, but it is to imitate Christ in everything, always and everywhere.

Why does Jesus insist upon our obligation to imitate Him? Perhaps because it is the duty of a disciple to imitate his master. Such a reply is evidently true because Jesus Himself gave it. But there is another answer, much deeper, which He gave on another occasion. The imitation which He demands of us is really incomparably more intimate and more complete than that of any ordinary disciple of any ordinary master. There is a mystery here that was unknown to the Jews of the Old Testament, unknown to the crowds who thronged about Jesus, unknown even to His intimates, the Twelve, up to the last hour before His Passion.

Certainly He had said to His audience that whatever was done to one of His least followers was done to Him (cf. Mt 25:40, 45). This identification might appear strange, but if a person reflected upon it, he would see in it only the great love of Jesus for His disciples. In the synagogue of Capharnaum He had been

1

more explicit, though still somewhat obscure, when He said: "As I live because of the Father, so he who eats me, he also shall live because of me" (Jn 6:58). But His hearers revolted from the prospect of having to eat His flesh and drink His blood, and His Apostles themselves were content to make an act of blind faith in their Master, without trying to understand how they were to eat His flesh and live on Him.

It was after having instituted the Eucharist and having given them His flesh to eat that He explained to them the mystery, as much as they were able to understand it at that time.

"I am the vine," He said to them, "you are the branches. He who abides in me, and I in him, he bears much fruit; for without me you can do nothing. . . . If you abide in me, and if my words abide in you, ask whatever you will and it shall be done to you" (Jn 15:5, 7). To the Father He said: "Yet not for these [disciples] only do I pray, but for those also who through their word are to believe in me, that all may be one, even as thou, Father, in me and I in thee; that they also may be one in us, that the world may believe that thou hast sent me. And the glory that thou hast given me, I have given to them, that they may be one, even as we are one: I in them and thou in me; that they may be perfected in unity, and that the world may know that thou hast sent me, and that thou hast loved them even as thou hast loved me. Father, I will that where I am, they also whom thou hast given me may be with me; in order that they may behold my glory, which thou hast given me, because thou hast loved me. . . . Just Father, the world has not known thee . . . and these have known that thou hast sent me. And I have made known to them thy name, and will make it known, in order that the love with which thou hast loved me may be in them, and I in them" (Jn 17:20–26).

Jesus therefore revealed to His disciples and to their successors a quasi identity between them and Him: He is the vine, they are its branches. The same sap flows through the vine and through the branches; the same life animates the trunk and the limbs. Hence, the union which exists between Him and the

Father exists between them and Him. His glory has become their glory; His knowledge of the Father, their knowledge; the love of the Father for the Son, the love of the Father for them; His dwelling with the Father, their dwelling with Him. He gave them all that He is and all that He has: His nature, His Father, His knowledge, His glory, His heaven, and He promised besides to send them His Spirit. The following day, from the cross He was also to give them His Mother. Can a closer identity be imagined between Him and them, between Him and us?

That revelation made by Jesus likens our condition to His. Christ is God made man; a Christian is man made God. Evidently there cannot be question here of an identity; the Word was united substantially only with the Son of Mary.

St. Peter states the point exactly: the Christian has become a *partaker* of the divine nature (2 Pt 1:4). We do not possess the divine nature; we partake of it, we share it. That is the condition of a precious stone exposed to the rays of the sun: it shines like the sun because it shares in its brilliance, but it does not possess that brilliance of itself. Such is also an iron bar in a furnace: it glows like fire, it heats like fire, it can light a flame like fire, but it only participates in those properties and can lose them. In the same way, the soul in the state of grace participates in the nature of God. It shares in His knowledge, His love, and His happiness; but it does not possess these gifts of itself and may lose them through mortal sin. Still, it depends upon the soul not to lose them, to hold fast to them, from the moment of baptism or of a good confession, until death and even throughout all eternity.

We have difficulty *realizing* this truth of our participation in the divine nature, because we do not know it from direct experience but only from faith, while at the same time experience allows us to see our body and our soul only with their weaknesses, deformities, and faults. But faith gives us the certitude of this truth, and if we try to realize our participation with Christ, we marvel. St. John the Apostle, a mystic par excellence, speaking of this mystery to the first Christians, cannot restrain his joy: "Behold what manner of love the Father has bestowed upon us, that we should be called children of God; and such we are [in reality]." This gift of the Father is so great, so unbelievably great, that the Apostle continues ecstatically: "Beloved, now we are the children of God, and it has not yet appeared what we shall be. We know that, when he appears, we shall be like to him, for we shall see him just as he is" (1 Jn 3:1–2).

Such a condescension, such a love of God for creatures, so imperfect and so ungrateful, demands of us, first of all, an act of contemplation that is sheer admiration and gratitude. What are all the most ravishing spectacles, all the marvelous treasures of this world in comparison with this fact, that I, a poor creature, a poor sinner, clinging to the things of this world, can really be a child of God, called to share with Him His life, His glory, His happiness throughout eternity, and that throughout eternity I shall bless Him for it. But, from now on I must often recall this divine vocation which the Father has given me, and which the Son, my Brother, has merited for me by His sufferings and death, in order to thank Them for it, and to enjoy it myself.

This love and condescendence of God demands still another thing of me, that I show myself worthy of such a vocation. *Noblesse oblige!* A king's son has not the right to act like the son of a slave. The Father did for me all that He could do, and His Son suffered all that He could suffer, to make of me another Christ. They have given me all that depended on Them. But, in turn, They ask of me all that depends on me in order to live really as Christ, the Son of God; and what depends on me is precisely the constant effort to reproduce all the dispositions of Christ, to make mine not only His nature, but His thoughts, His affections, His acts of will, all His actions. His Mother will help me in all this. He gave her to me, to teach me to live His life.

Chapter 2

CHRIST OUR LIFE, ACCORDING TO ST. PAUL

The habit of viewing our entire life and all our duties in the light of Christ is of extreme importance. Failure to understand this has made many lay people incapable of living habitually in the state of grace, and has caused many religious to remain in a state of mediocrity instead of reaching sanctity. To realize its importance, we must examine the marvels which the doctrine of our identification with Christ has produced wherever it has been understood, that is, in the early Church and among the saints. In the early Church, St. Paul furnishes us with the most information.

The Fact of Our Identification With Christ

Here, in bold outlines, is the doctrine of our identification with Christ, according to St. Paul. We are all dead spiritually because of the sin of Adam. Christ redeemed us and gave life back to us. "But where the offense has abounded, grace has abounded yet more" (Rom 5:20).

This life which Christ has given us again is His life as Son of God. "But when the fullness of time came, God sent His Son, born of a woman, born under the Law, that He might redeem those who were under the Law, that we might receive the adoption of sons. And because you are sons, God has sent the Spirit of his Son into our hearts, crying, 'Abba, Father'" (Gal 4:4-6). Without doubt, St. Paul is alluding to the mystic graces profusely accorded to the converts of his time, which rendered them conscious of the indwelling of God. He concludes: You are then "no longer a slave, but a son" (Gal. 4:7).

To explain to the Apostles the quasi identity that there was

5

between Him and them, Jesus used the comparison of the vine
and the branches. Paul compared the body and its members.
He wrote to the Corinthians: "You are the body of Christ, member for member" (1 Cor 12:27). And to the Ephesians: "Rather
are we to practice the truth in love, and so grow up in all things
in him who is the head, Christ. For from him the whole body
(being closely joined and knit together through every joint of
the system according to the functioning in due measure of each
single part) derives its increase to the building up of itself in
love" (Eph 4:15–16). The same blood circulates in the Head
and in the members, the same life animates them. Accordingly
each one of the faithful can exclaim with Paul: "It is now no
longer I that live, but Christ lives in me" (Gal 2:20). "For me
to live is Christ and to die is gain" (Phil 1:21).

Consequences of Our Identification With Christ

ATTITUDE OF A CHILD. Since we share in the condition of Christ,
we are sons of the same Father as He, and we must adopt a
completely childlike attitude toward the Father just as Christ
did. We have heard St. Paul explain that it is the Spirit of
Christ which makes us cry out to God, "Father, Father."

PERSEVERANCE IN THE LIFE OF CHRIST. Once we have received it, we must persevere in this life of Christ, that is, in the
state of grace. "All we who have been baptized into Christ Jesus
have been baptized into his death. For we were buried with
him by means of Baptism into death, in order that, just as
Christ has arisen from the dead through the glory of the Father,
so we also may walk in newness of life. . . . Thus do you
consider yourselves also as dead to sin, but alive to God in
Christ Jesus" (Rom 6:3–11). "There is therefore now no condemnation for those who are in Christ Jesus. . . . For the law
of the Spirit of the life in Christ Jesus has delivered me from
the law of sin and of death" (Rom 8:1–2). In Paul's eyes, the
disciples of Christ no longer commit grave sin. He knows well
that there are exceptions among them as there had been sins

even among the Twelve. But normally, they persevere in the life of grace, through the strength of Christ who lives in them. Like Paul they know that in temptation His grace is sufficient for them, because His strength is made perfect in their weakness, and it is when they are weak that they are strong (cf. 2 Cor 12:9–10).

THE GLORIOUS RESURRECTION OF OUR BODIES. In the next life, far more than in this, the condition of Christians will be similar to Christ's. Christ rose from the dead; they will rise like Him. St. Paul strongly affirms and proves it. Their condition is so identical to that of their Head that Paul dares argue: "If there is no resurrection of the dead, neither has Christ risen" (1 Cor 15:13).

PARTICIPATION IN THE HERITAGE OF CHRIST. Not only shall we rise like Christ; we shall share His inheritance, for "if we are sons, we are heirs also: heirs indeed of God and joint heirs with Christ" (Rom 8:17). "Our citizenship is in heaven from which also we eagerly await a Savior, our Lord Jesus Christ, who will refashion the body of our lowliness, conforming it to the body of his glory" (Phil 3:20–21).

CERTAINTY OF OUR SALVATION. We cannot be lost. "Who shall make accusation against the elect of God? It is God who justifies! Who shall condemn? It is Christ Jesus who died; yes, and rose again, he who is at the right hand of God, who also intercedes for us" (Rom 8:33–34).

We possess all the goods that we have because of Christ's love for us. Though we were His enemies, He died for us. "For scarcely in behalf of a just man does one die. . . . But God commends his charity towards us, because when as yet we were sinners, Christ died for us . . . much more, having been reconciled, shall we be saved by his life" (Rom 5:7–10). "Who shall separate us from the love of Christ [for us]? Shall tribulation, or distress, or persecution, or hunger, or nakedness, or danger, or the sword? . . . But in all these things we overcome because of him who has loved us. For I am sure that neither death, nor life, nor angels, nor principalities, nor things present, nor things to come, nor powers, nor height, nor depth, nor any other creature will be able to separate us from the love of God, which is in Christ Jesus our Lord" (Rom 8:35–39). "Thanks be to God who has given us the victory through our Lord Jesus Christ" (1 Cor 15:57). "If any man does not love the Lord Jesus Christ, let him be anathema. Maranatha [The Lord comes]" (1 Cor 16:22).

Are we surprised that men, only yesterday engulfed in the filth of paganism, hearing Paul tell in burning accents what marvels the love of Christ performed and would continue to perform for them, admitting them to participate in His nature and in all His divine grandeurs — are we surprised that they generously accepted and lived His doctrine regardless of sacrifice? And should we be astonished, if Christians today would begin to lead an altogether different life from what they are leading, if they could only realize these same marvels?

Chapter 3

OUR IMITATION OF THE LIFE OF CHRIST, ACCORDING TO ST. PAUL

We have seen according to St. Paul what Christ has done for us. Let us see with the same Apostle what we should do for Christ. We know it in general already: we must live only for Him and reproduce all His dispositions. Let us ponder what this program comprises in detail.

All for Jesus. Reproducing His Various Dispositions

All for Jesus. St. Paul is very precise in this matter. He wrote to the Romans, for instance: "If we live, we live to the Lord, or if we die, we die to the Lord. Therefore, whether we live or die, we are the Lord's. For to this end Christ died and rose again, that he might be Lord both of the dead and of the living" (Rom 14:8–9). And to the Colossians: "Whatever you do in word or in work, do all in the name of the Lord Jesus, giving thanks to God the Father through him" (Col 3:17).

We must not only work for Christ, we must become Christ who is acting through us. This is equivalent to leading an entirely new life, the life of Christ, with whom we form but one body. To the same Romans he explained: "Do you not know that all we who have been baptized into Christ Jesus have been baptized into his death? For we were buried with him by means of Baptism into death, in order that, just as Christ has arisen from the dead through the glory of the Father, so we also may walk in newness of life. For if we have been united with him in the likeness of his death, we shall be so in the likeness of his resurrection also" (Rom 6:3–5).

9

Living the life of Christ demands, according to St. Paul, reproducing all the perfections of Christ. We must "attain . . . to
the mature measure of the fullness of Christ" (Eph 4:13).[1] Each
of our dispositions must be modeled on the corresponding disposition of Christ.

MORTIFICATION. In his letter to the Galatians, St. Paul listed
the "desires of the flesh," that is, of nature not submitted to
grace: immorality, uncleanness, licentiousness, idolatry, enmities,
quarrels, etc., and he concluded: "They who belong to Christ
have crucified their flesh with its passions and desires" (Gal
5:19–23).

PURITY. Paul returned to this particular point on several occasions because of the depths to which the pagans descended
and to which a certain number of his converts had descended
in the past. In his epistle to the Romans he made this recommendation: "Let us walk becomingly as in the day, not in revelry
and drunkenness, not in debauchery and wantonness. . . . But
put on the Lord Jesus Christ, and as for the flesh, take no
thought for its lusts" (Rom 13:13–14). He wrote to the Corinthians more vehemently, and rightly so: "Do not err; neither
fornicators, nor idolaters, nor adulterers, nor the effeminate . . .
will possess the kingdom of God. And such were some of you,
but you have been washed, you have been sanctified, you have
been justified in the name of our Lord Jesus Christ, and in the
spirit of our God" (1 Cor 6:9–11). A little further on in forceful
words he continued: "Do you not know that your bodies are
members of Christ? Shall I then take the members of Christ
and make them members of a harlot? By no means! Or do you
not know that . . . he who cleaves to the Lord is one spirit with
him? . . . You have been bought at a great price. Glorify God
and bear him in your body" (1 Cor 6:15–17, 20).

OBEDIENCE AND HUMILITY. "Have this mind in you which was
also in Christ Jesus, who though he was by nature God, did not

---

[1] Perhaps the sense of this passage is that we must all grow in perfection
so as to form one perfect body with Christ, our Head. This meaning
scarcely differs from that of the previous passage, as regards the obligation to become like Christ.

consider being equal to God a thing to be clung to, but emptied himself, taking the nature of a slave and being made like unto men. And appearing in the form of man, he humbled himself, becoming obedient to death, even to death on a cross" (Phil 2:5-8).

THE SPIRIT OF POVERTY. "For you know the graciousness of our Lord Jesus Christ — how, being rich, he became poor for your sakes" (2 Cor 8:9).

Even in the natural relations among members of a family, Paul found a way to recall the example or the thought of Christ. Citing the line from Genesis, "A man leaves his father and mother, and clings to his wife, and the two become one flesh" (Gen 2:24), he explained: "This is a great mystery — I mean in reference to Christ and to the Church" (Eph 5:32). Then, speaking of the particular obligations of different members of the family, he wrote: "Husbands, love your wives, just as Christ also loved the Church, and delivered himself up for her" (Eph 5:25). "Let wives be subject to their husbands as to the Lord; because a husband is head of the wife, just as Christ is head of the Church" (Eph 5:22, 23). "Children, obey your parents in all things, for that is pleasing to the Lord. . . . Slaves, obey in all things your masters according to the flesh; not with eye-service seeking to please men, but in singleness of heart from fear of the Lord" (Col 3:20-26). "Masters, give your slaves what is just and fair, knowing that you too have a Master in heaven" (Col 4:1).

THE SPECIAL PRACTICE OF CHARITY IN CHRIST. St. Paul preaches, above all, the precept of charity. We recall the enthusiastic hymn of praise to charity, the virtue superior to all others and which summarizes them all (cf. 1 Cor 13:1-7; Rom 13:8-10). It results from our being but one with Christ. Paul loves to consider all Christians as forming only one body with Christ. "For as the body is one and has many members, and all the members of the body, many as they are, form one body, so also is it with Christ. For in one Spirit we were all baptized into one body, whether Jews or Gentiles, whether slaves or free;

and we were all given to drink of one Spirit" (1 Cor 12:12–13).
Previously he had made another comparison, that of the Eucha-
ristic Bread: "Because the bread is one, we though many, are
one body, all of us who partake of the one bread" (1 Cor 10:17).
Accordingly, anything good or bad that we do to another, we
do to Christ. All the recommendations that St. Paul makes about
charity result from these relations between Christ and His
disciples.

FRATERNAL UNION. "May then the God of patience and of
comfort grant you to be of one mind towards one another according to Jesus Christ; that, one in spirit, you may with one
mouth glorify the God and Father of our Lord Jesus Christ"
(Rom 15:5–6). Therefore, no discord. "Now this is what I
mean: each of you says, I am of Paul, or I am of Apollos, or
I am of Cephas, or I am of Christ. Has Christ been divided up?
Was Paul crucified for you?" (1 Cor 1:12).

FORGETFULNESS OF SELF FOR THE SAKE OF OTHERS. "Let every
one of you please his neighbor by doing good, for his edification;
for Christ did not please himself" (Rom 15:2–3). "Wherefore
receive one another, even as Christ has received you to the
honor of God. For I say that Christ Jesus has been a minister
of the circumcision in order to show God's fidelity in confirming
the promises made to our fathers, but that the Gentiles glorify
God because of his mercy" (Rom 15:7–9). "Bear one another's
burdens, and so you will fulfill the law of Christ" (Gal 6:2).

No SCANDAL TO OTHERS. A Christian should abstain from food
offered to false gods if those present would be scandalized.
He solemnly calls upon his Roman reader: "Do not with thy
food destroy him for whom Christ died" (Rom 14:15); and even
more forcefully he conjures the Corinthian reader: "And through
thy 'knowledge' [knowing that in itself the eating is indifferent]
the weak one will perish, the brother for whom Christ died.
Now when you sin thus against the brethren, and wound their
weak conscience, you sin against Christ" (1 Cor 8:11–12).

FORGIVENESS OF INJURIES. It will happen that Christians offend
their brethren. St. Paul advises them: "Be kind to one another,

and merciful, generously forgiving one another, as also God in Christ has generously forgiven you" (Eph 4:32).

Of course, all the disciples of Paul did not accept these instructions with the same docility. Many a time he had to reprimand them for their conduct. Reading his letters, however, you become convinced of the fervor of the majority in their practice of fraternal charity. He could write to almost all of them as he did to the Thessalonians: "We are bound to give thanks to God always for you, brethren. It is fitting that we should, because your faith grows exceedingly and your charity each one for the other increases" (2 Thes 1:3).

Besides, wherever they loved one another in Christ they practiced a charity that astonished the uninitiated. We recall that in the community of Jerusalem "the multitude of the believers were of one heart and one soul." St. Jerome makes the same remark of the Christians of Alexandria. And Tertullian reports that the astonished pagans exclaimed: "Look at the Christians how they love one another, while we tear each other to shreds!"[2]

Like charity, all the other virtues become, in a quite different manner, more attractive, easier, and more perfect, when they are viewed with St. Paul and the first Christians in the light of Jesus Christ.

---

[2] On the complete transformation of the moral conduct of the first Christians because of the thought of Christ, see Daniel Rops, *L'Eglise des Apotres et des Martyrs*, pp. 262–267.

Chapter 4

THE TESTIMONY OF ST. TERESA OF THE CHILD JESUS, THE LITTLE FLOWER

The Christocentric spirituality which St. Paul lived and preached with so much zeal and success in the first century proved itself just as effective in the nineteenth century in the life of St. Teresa of Lisieux. Here are telling proofs.

St. Teresa of the Child Jesus is preeminently the saint of the love of Jesus. All her sisters lived in the same family environment as she, profited by the same education, saw the same models of virtue, and all of them became fervent religious. Still, as far as can be judged, Teresa far surpassed them. Evidently she received the special grace from God to reduce everything to the love of Jesus, His love for her and her love for Him.

From the supernatural point of view, she was exceptionally precocious. From earliest childhood, she saw everything in religion under the form of love of Jesus. She recalled that from the age of three she had never refused Him anything.[1] Her mother relates how "a hundred times a day, putting her hand in her little pocket, she drew a pearl on her movable string of beads to mark each sacrifice."[2] Evidently it was for Jesus that she made her sacrifices. She prepared for her First Holy Communion by "a great number of sacrifices and acts of love."[3] "Oh, how sweet was that first kiss of Jesus on my soul," she wrote. "Yes, that was a kiss of love. I felt that I was loved, and I too said, 'I love You and I give myself to You forever. . . .' For a long time He and little Teresa had looked at and understood one another. That day our meeting could not be called any

---

[1] St. Teresa of Lisieux, Little Flower of Jesus, p. 266.
[2] Ibid., p. 14.
[3] Ibid.

14

longer a simple look but a *fusion*. We were no longer two; Teresa had disappeared like a drop of water in the ocean."[4]

At her second Communion the intimacy was even closer: "I recalled and repeated continually the words of St. Paul 'It is now no longer I that live, but Christ lives in me.' "[5]

For years she longed to become a nun so that she might belong entirely to Jesus. She could not wait to complete her union with Him. To enter Carmel sooner, on the occasion of her pilgrimage to Rome, despite the order to keep silence, she did not hesitate to ask the authorization from Leo XIII.

Finally her desire was realized; she became a Carmelite. In the postulate and novitiate, she had to read St. John of the Cross to acquire the spirit of Carmel. Soon all spiritual writers left her dry. She could read nothing else but Holy Scripture and the *Imitation of Christ*. But it was, above all, the Gospels that engaged her during her meditations. "There," she said, "I find everything that is necessary for my poor soul." From then on, night and day, she carried the Gospel on her heart. One day, Reverend Mother Agnes, her "little Mother," spoke to her of various practices of devotion or of perfection, recommended by certain spiritual writers, but which discouraged many souls. Teresa answered: "As far as I am concerned, I do not find anything in books, except in the gospels. That book is enough for me. I listen with pleasure to this word of Jesus that tells me everything I have to do: '*Learn of Me because I am meek and humble of heart.*' It gives me peace according to the promise, 'and you will find peace for your souls.' "[6]

In 1895 she received the favor of understanding better than ever that Jesus desires to be loved. She conceived the idea of offering herself as a victim to His love. During Mass on the feast of the Holy Trinity that year, she made her perpetual consecration to the merciful love of Jesus. "Oh, from that day on," she confessed to her Mother, "love penetrates and surrounds me;

---

[4] *Ibid.*, p. 59.
[5] *Ibid.*, p. 61.
[6] *Novissima Verba*, 8.

every moment that merciful love renews and purifies me, and
leaves no trace of sin in my heart. . . . No, I cannot fear purgatory.
. . . I know that the fire of love is more sanctifying than that of
purgatory, I know that Jesus cannot want useless sufferings from
me, and that He would not inspire me with the desires that I
have, if He did not want to fulfill them."[7]

Some days later, beginning the way of the cross, she was
suddenly wounded by a flame so ardent that she felt she would
die of it.

She had desired the death of Jesus crucified, and her prayer
was heard. Her sufferings were terrible, both physical and
spiritual, especially temptations against faith. "I would never
have thought that it was possible to suffer so much," she said.
"I can only explain that by my eagerness to save souls. . . . And
I certainly want to suffer more."[8]

Her agony began. Teresa fixed her gaze upon her crucifix.
She held it so tight, that after her death it could hardly be re-
moved. Her heavy breathing lasted two hours. At six o'clock the
Angelus rang, and the dying nun looked at the statue of the
"Virgin of the Smile" who had cured her in her childhood.
Then a last look at the crucifix and she murmured: "Oh, I
love You! My God . . . I . . . love . . . You!" Her face became
transfigured. After the space of a Credo she closed her eyes.
She had died of love.

Is not this method of St. Teresa of the Child Jesus, perfect
though it be, contrary to the common ascetical teaching and,
accordingly, only to be suggested to exceptional souls like St.
Teresa? Did not the saint by rare privilege skip the ordinary
stages of perfection? Before wishing to apply oneself to a life
of union with God, should not a person begin by learning self-
renouncement, to rid himself of his faults and defects, according
to the program called "the purgative way?" Then, in the "illumi-
native way" should he not apply himself to acquiring the vari-

---

[7] *St. Teresa of Lisieux*, p. 148 f.
[8] *Novissima Verba*, 194 f.

ous virtues? Did St. Teresa do all that? No, not in the usual way. But she did in a more perfect and a more rapid way.

Instead of making these different exercises of ascetical gymnastics her chief concern, and of scarcely thinking of our Lord except at vocal and mental prayer, she placed Jesus at the center of her entire life, of all her interests and of all her acts, even the natural ones. She found in this practice the most powerful motive and the greatest aid for mortification, for cleansing herself of all defects, for becoming recollected and for practicing all virtues. In trying not to refuse Jesus anything, from the age of three, did she not practice a continual mortification, a constant vigilance over herself in order not to permit herself anything which could displease her Divine Lover? Is not her little way of spiritual childhood the habitual practice of humility and simplicity? Did not her intimate contact with Jesus, the Savior, who revealed to her His infinite mercy, give her absolute confidence in Him, make her expect from His goodness without the least hesitation everything that she needed, and compel her unconditional surrender to Him? She herself admitted that this confidence did not result from the fact that she was preserved from mortal sin. "Oh," she cried out, "I feel Him, and even should I have on my conscience all the crimes that can be committed, I would lose none of my confidence; with a broken heart, I would go and throw myself into the arms of my Savior. . . . I know that all these sins would vanish in a twinkling, as a drop of water thrown upon a hot fire."[9]

And as to that virtue which surpasses all others and sums them up, fraternal charity, had she not learned from Jesus that, whatever one does to the least of His brethren one does to Him? Recall the incident of the nun who "had the talent to displease her in everything." Teresa tried to do for her what she would have done for the person she loved most. "Every time I met her, I prayed to God for her, offering Him all her virtues and merits. I was sure that that greatly pleased Jesus. . . . I was not content to pray for her who caused me so many struggles,

---

[9] *St. Teresa of Lisieux,* p. 205.

I tried to do as many favors as possible for her, and when I was tempted to answer her disagreeably, I was careful to give her a friendly smile. . . . On such an occasion, she said to me one day with a radiant air: 'Sister Teresa of the Child Jesus, please tell me, what draws you to me? I never meet you without your giving me your sweetest smile!' . . . Oh, what attracted me was Jesus hidden at the bottom of her soul, Jesus who makes what is bitter, most sweet."[10]

Every saint has his providential mission. That of St. Teresa of the Child Jesus is clear: it is to teach us her "little way," the "way of spiritual childhood." That way consists in going straight to Jesus in all simplicity and confidence, doing everything out of love for Him and expecting everything from His love for us. And Jesus has to be sought above all in the Gospel.

This quite simple and confident way to love Jesus not only offers, in the highest degree, all the aids toward perfection that can be found in the long and complicated practices of the traditional three ways, but actually led a young nun, who died at scarcely twenty-four, to the heights of sanctity. St. Pius X bore witness to this fact when he called her "the greatest saint of modern times."

---

[10] *Ibid.*, p. 172 f.

Chapter 5

TESTIMONY OF THE MASTERS OF THE SPIRITUAL LIFE

Together with St. Paul, the Christians of the first century, and St. Teresa of the Child Jesus, the greatest masters of the spiritual life of all ages also teach us of the exceptional efficacy of the spiritual life in which Jesus Christ is the beginning and the end, the goal and the means, the motive and the reward.

SAINT-JURE. "We must place this exercise of union with our Lord above all others, and make of it the center of our devotions. It happens often, and only too often in the spiritual life, that many scatter their efforts in petty practices and dissipate their attention in a variety of interests. This is not a good method, but rather annoying, and more apt to cause a soul to slip back on the way of perfection than to advance in it. It is like playing around in the branches, and leaving the trunk and the root. To do a good job, we have to reduce all things to unity, as much as possible, and to limit ourselves to a few important and solid interests, on which others are dependent and to which they are attached.

"Now I find that the only practice which has all these advantages is union with our Lord, which we should, therefore, adopt and eagerly embrace without tormenting ourselves or bothering much about the rest, endeavoring only to cultivate and to perfect this union by every possible means, making it more intimate day by day, and continually tightening the bond which unites us with Him.

"For this reason we should think only of acquiring this union. 'Martha, Martha, thou art anxious . . .' You engage in

19

many practices which of course are good; you spread yourself
out in many exercises of piety carefully and often eagerly, perhaps even with some pain. But there is one necessary above all
and that is to really unite yourself with Jesus Christ."¹

ST. JOHN EUDES. "When you wish to make progress in any
virtue: (1) Adore that virtue in Our Lord Jesus Christ and consider how He was eminent in it and how perfectly He practiced
it all His life. (2) Humble yourself before Him, seeing yourself
so far from that perfection, asking His pardon for all the faults
that you ever committed in practicing this virtue. . . . (3) Give
yourself often to Jesus with a great desire to practice the virtue
in all the perfection He demands of you, and beg Him to
destroy in you all that is contrary to the virtue, and to imprint
and establish it in you only for His glory. (4) Take care actually
to practice the virtue by interior acts and with exterior fruits,
uniting yourself to the dispositions and intentions with which
Jesus Christ practiced those same virtues. . . .

"When you commit a fault against the virtue, do not be
troubled or discouraged; instead, humble yourself before God,
asking His pardon and offering all the honor which His well-
beloved Son and His most holy Mother rendered Him by the
practice of that virtue, in reparation for your fault. Give yourself again to Jesus, with a renewed desire to be faithful to Him
in the future, in practicing the virtue, and beg Him in His great
mercy to repair your fault and to give you fresh grace to practice it better on the occasions that will present themselves."²

FATHER LALLEMANT. "There are persons who blindfold their
minds in order to rummage around for several motives to en-
rich their virtuous actions, thinking that, by so doing, they
render these actions more pleasing to God. We must simply try
to see what virtue God desires of us in each act, and then simply
perform that act in God's presence, with the intention that He
inspires and with the motive and purpose of imitating our Lord.

---

¹ *L'Union a Notre-Seigneur.*
² *Royaume de Jesus,* 2 part, n. 23; Lebrun, *Spiritualite de S. J. Eudes,*
p. 174.

"That is why the love of our Lord is so highly recommended as an easy motive, appropriate to everybody, wholesome and satisfying. And the good that we accomplish under the inspiration of such love, for example, an act of temperance done to imitate and to please our Lord, is far more excellent than an act done precisely to remain moderate as the virtue of temperance demands. . . .

"The apostles and the first Christians were full of Jesus. Love and imitation of Him were the ideal of perfection which they proposed to themselves, as can be seen in the Epistles of St. Paul. . . . True, virtues can be loved for their beauty and particular excellence, but considering their brilliance in the adorable person of the Son of God, we find them incomparably more lovable and more worthy of esteem. Such a view invests them with a divine splendor: in Jesus they are not only consecrated as they are in the saints; they are as it were deified."[3]

BISHOP HEDLEY, O.S.B., OF NEWPORT, ENGLAND. "It is a deep mistake to suppose that the best progress is made by efforts to acquire virtues and to root out vices. Such efforts must be made; but there is another and a better way (which at the same time does not dispense us from making efforts). That other way is the contemplative union of our intelligence, will, and heart with the Sacred Humanity of Jesus Christ. For that Sacred Humanity has a most powerful, and almost miraculous, efficacy of transformation. . . . An hour, or half an hour, of devout contemplation of His obedience, His patience, His humility, His love of suffering, will change our poor natures for the better more effectively than many days of striving to practice these virtues, were such practice unaccompanied by the contemplation here described. . . . Thus the saints have found, in prayer before the Sacred Humanity, their book, their lesson, their mirror, their transformation."[4]

DOM COLUMBA MARMION. "These souls that have not understood the mystery of Christ lose themselves in a multiplicity of

---

[3] Le Coffre, *La Doctrine Spirituelle du P. L. Lallemant.*
[4] John Cuthbert Hedley, O.S.B., *A Retreat*, pp. 129–132.

details and often weary themselves in a joyless labor. Why is this? Because all that our human ingenuity is able to create for our inner life serves for nothing if we do not base our edifice upon Christ: 'for other foundation no one can lay, but that which has been laid, which is Christ Jesus' (1 Cor 3:11).

"This explains the change that sometimes takes place in certain souls. For years, their lives have been as it were cramped, they have been often depressed, hardly ever contented, forever finding new difficulties in the spiritual life. Then one day God gives them the grace of understanding that Christ is our All, that He is the *Alpha* and *Omega* (Ap 22:13), that outside of Him we have nothing, that in Him we have everything, for everything is summed up in Him. From that moment all is, as it were, changed for these souls; their difficulties vanish like the shades of night before the rising sun. As soon as Our Lord, the true Sun of our lives, 'the Sun of justice' (Mal 4:2), fully illumines these souls, they unfold, mount upwards and bear much fruit of holiness. . . .

"The contemplation of Our Lord is not only holy but sanctifying: even only to think of Him, to look at Him with faith and love, sanctifies us. For certain souls, the life of Jesus Christ is one subject of meditation among many others; this is not enough. Christ is not one of the means of spiritual life; He is *all* our spiritual life. . . .

"Spiritual life consists above all in contemplating Christ, so that we may reproduce in ourselves His state of Son of God and His virtues. Those souls who constantly keep their eyes fixed on Christ see, in His light, all that in them is opposed to the expansion of the divine life; they then seek in Jesus the strength to put away these obstacles so as to please Him; they ask Him to be the support of their weakness, to give, and ever to increase in them, that fundamental disposition — in which lies all holiness — of always seeking to do that which is pleasing to His Father. . . .

"The riches of the grace Christ communicates to us are so great — St. Paul declares them unfathomable, *Investigabiles divitiae Christi* — that the sacraments are never exhausted. Outside the sacraments Christ still acts and operates in us. How is this? By the contact we have with Him in faith.

"In order to understand this, let us read again an episode related by St. Luke. In one of His apostolic journeys, our Divine Savior is surrounded and pressed by the multitude. A sick woman, desiring to be healed, approaches Him, and full of confidence, touches the hem of His garment. Immediately, Our Lord asks those who surround Him: 'Who is it that touched me?' And Peter answers: 'Master, the multitude throng and press thee, and dost thou say, Who touched me?' But Jesus insists: 'Somebody hath touched me; for I know that virtue has gone out from me.' And at that very instant the woman was healed: and this, on account of her faith: 'Thy faith has saved thee' (Lk 8:43–48).

"Something analogous takes place for us also. Each time that, even outside the sacraments, we approach Christ, a strength, a Divine virtue goes out from Him and penetrates our souls to enlighten and help them.

"You know the means of approaching Him is faith. By faith, we touch Christ, and at this Divine contact, little by little, our soul is transformed."[5]

We could also cite as witnesses the names of all the great reformers or authors of a profound renewal of Christian life and piety throughout the history of the Church: Benedict, Francis of Assisi, Ignatius of Loyola; then there were Berulle and his numerous disciples such as Condren, Boudon, John Eudes, Louis de Montfort, Chaminade; and then St. Alphonsus Liguori, Père Chevrier, and so on. To restore Christian life whose fire seemed to have gone out, to make it suddenly blaze up in hungry flames ready to set the universe afire, they instinctively turned toward Jesus, the Jesus of the Gospel. They contemplated Him, they studied Him, they became intoxicated with Him, they tried to reproduce Him in themselves, and they taught their disciples to contemplate and copy Him. These latter burned with the same fire as their masters. But after a while they became at-

---
[5] Marmion, *Christ, the Life of the Soul*, pp. 28, 60–61, 73.

tached only to words and to exterior practices and fell back into the lukewarmness of the Christians of other days. They must come back to Christ; He is as powerful today as He was in the periods of great fervor.

Chapter 6

WITH MARY TO CONTEMPLATE JESUS

With Mary at one's side, with her eyes, with her mind, and with her heart we should contemplate Jesus.

What reasons have we to unite with Mary in our contemplation of Jesus? Is it only because of filial piety that we do everything with her? Without doubt that need may exist, but we have other reasons for doing so, serious reasons, both supernatural and natural.

The principal reasons have been given us by St. Pius X. Having announced from the beginning of his pontificate that he was going "to restore all things in Christ," he saw that the best way to lead us to Christ was through His Mother. "For," he asked, "who does not hold it as an established fact that there is no surer or easier way than Mary for men to come to Jesus and to obtain, through Jesus, that perfect adoption of sons which makes us holy and without stain in the eyes of God?

"Certainly it was truly said to the Blessed Virgin, 'Blessed is she who has believed, because the things promised her by the Lord shall be accomplished,' namely, that she would conceive and bear the Son of God. If, consequently, she welcomed into her womb Him who by nature is Truth, in such a way that begotten in a new order and by a new birth — invisible in Himself, He makes Himself visible in our flesh (St. Leo) — from the moment that the Son of God is the author and the consummator of our faith, it is absolutely necessary that Mary be called a participant of the divine mysteries and in a way their guardian, and that in consequence upon her also, as upon the noblest foundation after Christ, the faith of all the ages rests.

"How could it be otherwise? Could not God have given us by

another way than Mary the Redeemer of humanity and the Founder of our faith? But since it pleased the Eternal Providence that the God-man be given us by the Blessed Virgin, and since she had conceived Him by the fecund power of the Holy Spirit, and actually carried Him in her womb, what remains except that we receive Jesus from the hands of Mary?"[1]

Therefore, the first reason is: it was God's will to give us Jesus through Mary. Another reason: it is Mary who knew Jesus best.

"To lead us to the knowledge of Jesus belongs to the Blessed Virgin, and above all to her. This is beyond all doubt, if one considers, among other things, that she alone in this world, under the same roof and in intimate familiarity, had those close relations which are implied between a mother and son. . . . The wonderful mysteries of the nativity and infancy of Jesus, those especially which refer to His Incarnation, the principle and foundation of our faith — to whom have they been more completely unveiled than to His mother? *She kept in mind and considered in her heart* what she had seen of His acts at Bethlehem, what she had seen in the temple of Jerusalem; but initiated still more into His intentions and into the secret plans of His will, she lived, you could say, the very life of her Son. No, there is no better teacher and guide to make Jesus known than Mary.

"From this it follows, as we have already suggested, that neither is there anyone her equal for uniting men with Jesus. If, indeed, according to the doctrine of the Divine Master Himself, 'This is everlasting life, that they may know thee, the only true God, and him whom thou hast sent, Jesus Christ' (Jn 17:3), then, just as we come to the knowledge of Jesus through Mary, so through her also it is easier for us to attain the life of which He is the principle and the source."[2]

Mary's mission as Mediatrix, as Dispensatrix of all graces is a further reason for our contemplating Jesus in union with her.

St. Pius X proves this mission and then concludes: "Who will not recognize that we have justly affirmed of Mary, since she

---

[1] *Maria*, III, 767.
[2] *Ibid.*, III, 767 f.

was the close companion of Jesus from the house of Nazareth to the hill of Calvary, initiated more than any other into the secrets of His heart, Dispensatrix as with motherly rights of the treasures of His merits, that she is, for all these reasons, a most certain and most efficacious help in attaining the knowledge and love of Jesus?"[3]

The final proof of St. Pius X is that of experience. "Those men, alas, who, seduced by the wiles of the demon or deceived by false doctrines, think they can do without the help of the Blessed Virgin by their conduct furnish us with a convincing proof. Unfortunate are they who neglect Mary under the pretext of rendering more homage to Jesus! As if one could find the Child elsewhere than with His Mother!"[4]

To these reasons can be added the consideration that, once she became the Mother of Christ and our Mother, Mary had to take care of the education of her children. But to raise us is to make us like Jesus, our older Brother. She has, consequently, a special grace, a *maternal* grace, to enable us to live the thoughts, the sentiments, the aspirations, the volitions of Jesus.

Moreover, to reveal her Son to us is for her a great joy, as Mother of Jesus and our mother. As Mother of Jesus, nothing is closer to her heart than to have Him known and loved who is the sole reason for her existence; as our mother, she desires nothing so much for us as to see us become like to Him. How, then, could she not help us with all her power and love, to know and to reproduce Jesus her Son in ourselves?

These reasons are supernatural; there are others which are natural, psychological reasons.

Jesus is at the same time God and man. Without any doubt, He has everything that a man has; He became "as we are in all things except sin" (Heb 4:15). But He is at the same time God, and when there is question of imitating Him we can use the pretext that such or such a human disposition of His has to be sustained by the divinity: how could we reproduce it? Mary is a

---

[3] *Ibid.,* 770.
[4] *Ibid.*

pure creature and she has reproduced everything in her Son
that a pure creature could. Contemplating that disposition in
both Jesus and Mary, we can more easily see just what in Him
we also can reproduce. Thus, to contemplate Jesus we understand Him better in contemplating Mary also.

Jesus is a masterpiece written in a language that we understand only imperfectly. Mary is the translation into our language.
A translation has not the value of the original but it helps us
better to divine the beauties of the original.

A translation sometimes falsifies certain lines of the original:
a proverb puts it thus, *traduttore, traditore,* that is, "translator,
traitor." St. Paul, who according to his own avowal tried constantly to imitate Christ (cf. 1 Cor 4:16, 11, 1; Phil 3:17), does
not always speak as Christ would have spoken, but according
to his own temperament (Gal 5:12; 1 Cor 11:5–6; Acts 23:3;
24:10). With Mary the case is different: conceived without sin,
free from all concupiscence, she was not tainted by the disorder
that original sin introduced even into the nature of the saints.
She is in perfect equilibrium and harmony as is her Son, and
she was never exposed as we have been to deforming the traits
that she copied from Him.

Besides, since according to the law of nature children reproduce the characteristics of their parents, and since He drew His
humanity from Mary alone, God made her so, as He wished her
to make His Son. "Grace in forming Mary," explained Father
Chaminade, "took as model Jesus Christ, and the august Virgin
is so perfect and so agreeable in God's eyes only because of her
resemblance, as perfect as possible, to Him with whom the Most
High was eternally well pleased. To imitate Mary, is then the
surest, swiftest and easiest means to imitate Jesus Christ."[5]

From another point of view, a child, as if by a special instinct,
understands what passes in the soul of his mother: joys, sorrows,
wishes, fears, ambitions. And it is also peculiarly easy for him
to reproduce what he senses in the mind of his mother. It is
possible that pondering a saying of Jesus or one of His actions,

---

[5] Chaminade, *The Spirit of Our Foundation,* I, 158.

my mind has no particular reaction, my heart remains cold, my will is unmoved. Still, I may easily enough be aware of how that word or that act affects Mary, so perfectly attuned to the soul of Jesus, and I can at least surmise something of what must have been her thoughts, her feelings, and her wishes. Contemplating her affectionately, and praying her to make my soul experience something of the thoughts and feelings which I perceive in hers, I sense that I, too, enter into the interior of her Son and begin "to have this mind in me which was also in Christ Jesus," to reproduce the dispositions of Jesus Christ.

Our contemplation of the soul of Jesus is more attractive and more loving, more penetrating, more understanding, more delicate, easier, and more rapid, and also surer, more efficacious and transforming, if it is done under the direction of Mary.

In this connection, here is a page from a renowned theologian who has meditated at some length on the mystery of Mary.

THE MARIAN MODALITY OF THE CHURCH. "There is a modality which grace received from the beginning and in an intense manner in the Blessed Virgin, and which it now has in the Church in such a way that one can say that the Church is Marian.

"This means that the Church spontaneously and even without thinking about it, looks at the mysteries of the Christian revelation with the eyes of Mary. The Church knows that Mary looked at these things before we did. What the Church finds in the mysteries of the Annunciation, of Christmas, of the Redemption on the cross, of Easter, of the Ascension, and of Pentecost is exactly what Mary saw in them. The faith of Mary forever colors the faith of the Church.

"With your own powers try to contemplate the mystery of the crib or that of the cross. Only after that, try to imagine what they meant to Mary of the Gospel, with what eyes she saw them. You will understand then what was missing in your first contemplation. And you will perhaps be able to imagine what those sects miss which refuse to borrow Mary's eyes when they read the revelation of the Gospel."[6]

---

[6] Chas Journet, L'Eglise du Verbe Incarne, Vol. II, p. 431.

Chapter 7

THE HOLY SPIRIT REVEALING JESUS

The Master is with His Apostles in the Cenacle. Judas has left the room and everyone feels at ease. Jesus has just given Himself as food and drink to His dear friends and has just made them the first priests.

It is the moment of the last farewells before the Passion. Jesus pours out His heart to His intimates, telling them all that is left to be told — His most precious mysteries. They are moved and sad beyond words because He is leaving them. But He promises them another envoy from His Father, who will take His place and remain ever with them, the Holy Spirit, the Paraclete; that is to say, someone who will come to support and console them. Five different times He mentions that name (Jn 14:16-17, 25; 15:26; 16:7-10, 12-15).

"Many things yet I have to say to you, but you cannot bear them now. But when he, the Spirit of truth, has come, he will teach you all the truth. For he will not speak on his own authority, but whatever he will hear he will speak, and the things that are to come he will declare to you. He will glorify me, because he will receive of what is mine and declare it to you. All things that the Father has are mine. That is why I have said that he will receive of what is mine, and will declare it to you" (Jn 16:12-15).

That prediction was to be realized in a wonderful way some weeks later, in consequence of the descent of the Holy Spirit on the day of Pentecost. The Apostles were assembled again in the Cenacle and Mary was with them. They prayed. Now there was a noise as of a great wind that filled the house and a tongue of fire rested upon the head of each one of them and all were

30

filled with the Holy Spirit. In a moment they were completely transformed. The Holy Spirit began to initiate them into the whole truth, that is to say, to reveal to them those truths which were still obscure, and He continues to do that until the end of the world, making successive generations see, little by little, truths hardly even suspected by the first disciples, such as, the glories of Mary; that is to say also, He initiated the disciples into truths about which heretofore they had false ideas, above all, about Christ's mission and about the true values of life. Up to the very day of the Ascension they had believed that He would drive out the Romans and reestablish the Kingdom of Israel which should dominate the entire world. With the coming of the Holy Spirit they understood that the kingdom consisted in the union of the disciples accepting the teachings and the authority of Christ. The sufferings and humiliations which the Messias had on several occasions foretold about Himself had always shocked them, so that one day Peter protested to Jesus: "Far be it from thee, O Lord; this will never happen to thee." The Master answered him indignantly: "Get behind me, satan, thou art a scandal to me; for thou dost not mind the things of God, but those of men" (Mt 16:22). After Pentecost, all the Apostles affirmed that it was by His Passion and His humiliations that Christ redeemed the world and established His kingdom. For them, too, suffering endured for the sake of Jesus was a cause of happiness. Formerly, and right up to the eve of the Passion, they entertained ambitions of mundane glory, and bickered about their claims to the first places. Now, there were no more clashes about rank. They had no other ambition than to suffer abuse for the name of Jesus (cf. Acts 5:41).

The Holy Spirit was to bring to the Apostles not only enlightenment for their minds but also strength for their wills. Shortly before ascending to His Father, Jesus had promised them: "You shall receive power when the Holy Spirit comes upon you, and you shall be witnesses for me in Jerusalem and in all Judea and Samaria and even to the very ends of the earth" (Acts 1:8).

This was to be evident from the day of Pentecost. When the Jews gathered around the Cenacle, Peter, who had recently quailed before a maidservant and denied His Master before a few domestics, now, together with the eleven, who had also been craven cowards since the Passion, presented himself boldly before the crowd, rebuked them for having had Jesus put to death at the hands of infidels, and charged them to change their hearts.

Three thousand of them accepted the religion of Jesus. Some time after, Peter and John were hailed before the Great Council, for having cured a lame man in the name of Jesus. In the presence of the highest authorities of the nation, they boldly confessed their faith in Christ, and when under menace they were charged to quit preaching, they protested that it was wiser to obey God than men. The affair of the deacon Stephen was even more striking. All the Pharisees and doctors together could not withstand the power and eloquence of the young disciple because he was "full of the Holy Spirit" (Acts 7:55).

This revelation of Jesus which the Holy Spirit made to the Apostles, He wishes to make also to their followers until the end of time. "He shall remain with you always," Jesus had promised. He remained with the first Christians and that is why Jesus was truly their all: by Him and for Him they lived, and for Him they died. It has ever been the same with Christians animated with a strongly Christocentric spirituality.

It is the Holy Spirit who gives us faith in Jesus. "No one can say 'Jesus is Lord,' except in the Holy Spirit" (1 Cor 12:3).

It is the Holy Spirit who makes us not only admit, but *realize* that we are sons of God. In his epistle Paul says to the Romans: "Now you have not received a spirit of bondage so as to be again in fear, but you have received a spirit of adoption as sons, by virtue of which we cry, 'Abba! Father!'" (Rom 8:15.) The Holy Spirit is not content to have us admit this fact as a truth of faith; He gives us a certain experience of it. St. Paul explains that the Holy Spirit unites Himself to our minds to give testimony that we are children of God (Rom 8:16). To the faithful, favored with mystical graces in receiving the Holy Spirit — and they were numerous in those first days of Christianity — He infuses a consciousness of their adoption. To others not so favored, He gives a quasi certitude of their adoption, by the sense of supernatural peace which they experience in their intimacy with God.

In these personal relations with God, it is the Holy Spirit who dictates what we should say. "But in like manner the Spirit also helps our weakness. For we do not know what we should pray for as we ought, but the Spirit himself pleads for us with unutterable groanings. And he who searches the hearts knows what the Spirit desires, that he pleads for the saints according to God" (Rom 8:26–27).

It is also the Holy Spirit who brings about fraternal union among the faithful. Each one has his special gift, and these gifts are varied, though all come from the same Spirit. "For as the body is one and has many members, and all the members of the body, many as they are, form one body, so also is it with Christ. For in one Spirit we were all baptized into one body, whether Jews or Gentiles, whether slaves or free; and we were all given to drink of one Spirit" (1 Cor 12:12–14).

This life under the direction of the Holy Spirit gives birth to a great joy. For what is more stimulating than to know or to feel that we are all children of God, brothers of Jesus Christ, and like Him heirs of our heavenly Father? The Acts of the Apostles, speaking of the faithful of Antioch of Pisidia, remark that they were "filled with joy and with the Holy Spirit" (Acts 13:52). But it is St. Paul who most insists on the joy that we experience in docility to the Holy Spirit. To the Romans he writes: "The kingdom of God does not consist in food and drink, but in justice and peace and *joy in the Holy Spirit*" (Rom 14:17). And again: "May the God of hope *fill you with all joy* and peace in believing, that you may abound in hope and in the power of the Holy Spirit" (Rom 15:13). He congratulates the Thessalonians: "You became imitators of us and of the Lord, receiving the word in

great tribulation, *with joy of the Holy Spirit,* so that you became
a pattern to all the believers in Macedonia and in Achaia" (1
Thes 1:6–7).

This marvelous action of the Holy Spirit supposes in the faithful a deep interior spirit to hear His inspirations, a spirit of
humility and docility to follow them. Paul recommended to the
Galatians: "If we live by the Spirit, by the Spirit let us also
walk" (Gal 5:25). And to the Ephesians: "Do not grieve [by
disobedience] the Holy Spirit of God, in whom you were sealed
for the day of redemption" (Eph 4:30). "Be filled with the Spirit,
speaking to one another in psalms and hymns and spiritual songs,
singing and making melody in your hearts to the Lord" (Eph
5:18–19).

In those days all the faithful venerated the Father and lived
for and by the Son under the inspiration of the Holy Spirit. In
our day to many of the faithful, even to the more religious, the
Holy Spirit is the Great Unknown, the Great Misunderstood, and
consequently the Father and the Son no longer appeal to them.

Mary wishes to lead us to the Holy Spirit as she leads us to
Jesus. It was by the descent of the Holy Spirit upon her that
she became the Mother of the Son of God. To have the same
Holy Spirit descend upon the Apostles, she prayed with them
during the ten days of the retreat in the Cenacle. With what
joy she must have observed the miraculous transformation which
the Holy Spirit worked in them, and, shortly after, in the
thousands of followers who embraced the religion of her Son!
She will also pray for us and with us, that we live by the same
Spirit, and that He grant us to know the Father, the Son, and
Himself, the Spirit of the Father and the Son.

> Through Thee may we the Father know,
> Through Thee the Eternal Son,
> And Thee the Spirit of them both,
> Thrice Blessed Three in One!

Chapter 8

PRACTICAL ADVICE

In the following chapters various states of the soul of Jesus will be studied according to the data of the Gospels. Each consideration will be followed by a study of the way Mary imitated that disposition of Jesus, and how we can and should follow their example.

It seems useful here to suggest a few ways to make these meditations practical. It is understood that the reader is free to choose; he may take or leave them. The truth to believe is one thing; but the various ways in which it can be lived are unlimited. Much depends on each person's temperament and character, on his happy or unhappy experiences, on his spiritual progress, his vocation, and so on.

From the suggestions that are offered, take what is useful here and now. We will never exhaust the contemplation of Jesus: we can return to it forever. It may be that the twentieth time you come back to consider a certain disposition of His, you will be struck by an aspect that left you completely indifferent the nineteen previous times. If, following one of the suggestions of this little book, you allow Mary to guide you in the contemplation of the soul of her divine Son, you will detect more easily what you should take for the present and what you should reserve for later.

In this study of the soul of Jesus, the principal data furnished by the Gospels have been brought together. The same procedure has been followed in contemplating a given disposition of the soul of Mary. Each of the following chapters may be read in a single sitting, but the reader might also pause at a stimulating

word or at an interesting act of Jesus or Mary, and reserve the
rest for one or more subsequent contemplations, following his
mood.

We are speaking of a contemplation of the soul of Jesus, not
of a psychological or theological study. We contemplate, not so
much to know as to love and to imitate. To contemplate we must
place ourselves in those dispositions that are favorable to
contemplation.

First, we need *recollection* in order to be able to focus our
minds and our hearts on Jesus and His Mother. Because of a
lack of real recollection many Christians, otherwise well disposed, remain, as it were, at the surface of these heavenly
models, and never experience just what it is to love Jesus and
to be one with Him.

Above all we need *love*. Jesus and Mary are pure love; everything about them is explained by love. To understand love, we
must know how to love.

To know how to love requires, first of all, renouncing everything opposed to love, namely sin, especially attachment to sin.
A serious sin, committed in an unguarded moment, once truly
repented, is no obstacle to love; it may even be the occasion
of an intensification of love. Such was the case with St. Peter.
But all selfishness in light matters, which we are unwilling to
sacrifice, renders love utterly impossible. "You cannot serve two
masters."

Understanding love requires, above all, positive acts of love,
especially those based on faith, which merit intimacy with Jesus.
We must make real what faith teaches us about union with
Christ, and be aware that we can say with St. Paul: "It is now
no longer I that live, but Christ lives in me." "For me to live
is Christ." By His divinity Jesus is intimately united to me;
I am more completely penetrated by Him than a red-hot iron
is with fire. Even by His humanity, He is more present to me
than a friend at my side, thanks to the Beatific Vision and, without doubt, thanks to a direct, mysterious influence of His humanity upon me. Mary also is more closely present to me than

a mother can be to the child she is carrying in her arms.[1] Now
it is with all their love that Jesus and Mary are present to me
when I think of them, and even when I forget or neglect them.
We must frequently renew this faith in their presence to make
it a habit. We should think of our Lord's presence when assisting
at Holy Mass, receiving Communion, or making spiritual Com-
munions. It is proper during the course of the day to think of
Mary's presence before saying the rosary or other prayers to
her. It is better to say only one decade of the beads in loving
union with Mary, according to the mystery of the decade, than
to say five without a moment of real contact with her.

When we begin to contemplate Jesus and Mary, it is important, for just a moment, to renew our faith in their loving
presence. It will be very useful to make a spiritual communion
directed toward the particular disposition that we wish to contemplate in Jesus. If it is humility, a prayer like this might be in
order: "Jesus, meek and humble of heart, come to me to give
me a share in Your humility. You have said: 'He who eats my
flesh will live by me.' I desire to receive You; make me live Your
humility." Like certain spiritual souls, we can make a sort of
"Marian Communion," that is to say, an aspiration to Mary asking for such or such a disposition as she had.[2]

To be most efficacious, this contemplation of the soul of Jesus
is made during prayer.

IN PRAYERS OF PETITION, we request Jesus to reveal to us His
dispositions, to make us love and imitate them, to show us how
His Mother understood, loved, and imitated them.

We petition the Holy Spirit to make us enter into the complete
reality of Christ; that we understand it, have a taste for it, love
it, practice it; in other words, that we become other Christs.

We ask Mary to teach us Jesus in order to live Him, and to
teach us how she learned and lived those truths.

We should address similar petitions to our guardian angel
and to other patrons.

---

[1] Cf. E. Neubert, *Life of Union With Mary*, pp. 43–46.
[2] Cf. *ibid.*, pp. 47 ff., 207 f.

IN THE PRAYER OF FAITH. Make many acts of faith. To believe
is to think the thoughts of Jesus. It is also to think the thoughts
of Mary. "I believe; Lord, help Thou my unbelief!" "O Mary,
Virgin most faithful, congratulated by the Holy Spirit for having believed, obtain for me the grace to believe as you believed in order to live as you lived."

IN THE PRAYER OF PRAISE, we admire the wonders of the mystery that is Jesus, of the mystery that is Mary, of the mystery of
our vocation to the divine life, and of all the choice, entirely
gratuitous, graces of which we have been the objects, despite
our resistance to the advances of Jesus and Mary.

These different kinds of prayer may be expressed in formulas,
but ordinarily they should be as brief as possible. Usually an
interjection is more laden with meaning than a pretty phrase.
The holy names of Jesus, Mary, my Mother, Holy Spirit, and
the like, are often more effective for putting us in the closest
contact possible with the divine Persons and with Mary, and
that without interrupting the contemplation.[3]

Here in this book we have been speaking of Jesus and Mary
in the third person. How could we do otherwise? In direct
contact with them, it is often advantageous to use the second
person. The text will say: "Jesus said to His disciples: 'If you
do not become as little children . . . !'" In my contemplation
nothing prevents me from saying: "Jesus, You whom I have
received this morning, or whom I shall receive tomorrow morning, or who is present here in the tabernacle, You said to Your
disciples, 'If you do not become as little children . . .'" In the
third person, Jesus and Mary are likely to remain people who
lived in Palestine two thousand years ago, or who are enthroned
in the highest heavens. In the second person, they are standing
before me, they act in me, and accordingly they are incomparably more lovable.

In the study of the soul of Jesus, we must of necessity limit

---

[3] Cf. *ibid.*, Chap. II.

ourselves, though the matter is inexhaustible. We have wished above all to suggest possible methods for this study. "The task of a good teacher is to teach the students to do without the teacher." We have a similar idea in this book, to teach the reader to pass up the book and to go directly to Jesus in the Gospels. You look at a painting by a talented artist, admire its fine points, then pass on never to return to it. What is the use? You saw whatever there was original that he had to offer. Before a masterpiece, on the contrary, you remain hours, and return gladly, because on each visit you find new beauties. The Gospel is the masterpiece of masterpieces. It is eminently the treasure house from which you can draw, without limit, things new and old. You never finish rereading because you never finish understanding, loving, and living Jesus.

This book might provide subjects for community meditation, through a choice of appropriate passages. Today, many persons prefer to meditate upon one or the other characteristic selection of a book rather than upon "points" which divide truth or reality rather artificially. For a resolution, it is only natural to imitate that aspect of the soul of Jesus or of His Mother viewed in the meditation. For a "spiritual bouquet" there is ample provision in the texts of the Gospel.

Instead of trying methodically to imitate each of the dispositions of the soul of Jesus, a person could, according to his inclinations, use the descriptions of them simply as means of entering into our Lord's soul, to admire its delicacy, its strength, above all its love, in order to be won over to it, to be immersed in it, penetrated by it, to live in intimacy with it as the Apostles did, particularly as John and Mary did. Jesus, contemplated in this way, will be identified with Jesus in one's daily life, because it is true for us as for St. Paul, *"for me to live is Christ."*

Let us illustrate this practically, according to the disposition of Jesus who is under contemplation. "Jesus, You who prayed to the Heavenly Father with such childlike submission . . ."; or "Jesus, You who pardoned Mary Magdalen . . . who raised

the son of the widow of Naim . . . You are the same Jesus whom
I received this morning . . . or last Sunday . . . so coldly, whom
I have crucified by my sins, who pardoned every one of them,
who calls me to follow You as closely as possible . . . that
Jesus whom I have just hurt by those thoughts of vanity, that
impatient word to one of my fellows . . . that same Jesus to
whom I pray so often with indifference, neglect, distractions.
Oh, I recite pretty formulas, all right, but my vain thoughts
or my personal, pet projects interest me more than You do. You
are He, who gave me Mary as mother, who inspired me with
great confidence in her, with the desire to imitate Your filial
piety toward her, who made me so happy in my relations with
her.

"Isn't it You also who ask that sacrifice of me which is so
frightening? I put off the inspiration with 'Oh, that's just imagination' or with 'There's really no strict obligation to do it.'
Isn't it You, nevertheless, who return to the charge with such
insistence, You who allowed Yourself to be crucified for me,
You who in Holy Communion give Yourself entirely, without
reserve to me? If it is You, what can I really answer except,
'Jesus, I will do all that You wish just because You want it, no
matter what it costs'?

"In just a moment, like yesterday, I will have to deal with such
and such a person. Yesterday it was boring. How shall I act
today? What I do to my neighbor is done to You, isn't it? Dear
Mother, help me to act toward this person as I would to Jesus
Himself.

"Throughout the day, in my various occupations, I think of
all sorts of futile things, of things past and future, of those accomplished and those which never will be done. And You, Jesus,
the one, great reality, my happiness in this life and in the next,
when does Your image ever come to my mind? Hours pass without a thought of You, and still You are in my soul; it is no
longer I who live, it is You who live in me.

"Mary, my Mother and Mother of Jesus, make me love Him
with your heart, and then, as He is with you, He will be present

in all my work. How shall I bring Jesus into every single act of my day . . . ?"

By such an identification of the Gospel Jesus with Jesus in my life, my entire day, my whole life, will be lived with this Jesus whom I contemplate under the direction of Mary. Without applying myself to imitate as perfectly as possible each of the dispositions of Jesus, I shall arrive at slowly putting Jesus into all that I think and feel and wish and do, at making my own all the feelings of Christ, "having this mind in me which was also in Christ Jesus" (Phil 2:5).

In the contemplation of the soul of Jesus, we shall first consider His soul in itself, then in its relations with the heavenly Father, and, finally, in its relations with men.

By the soul of Jesus in itself we mean His nature, His powers, the ways in which He is influenced. We are not here proposing a study of psychology, but a reverent contemplation of what we find admirable and imitable in His soul. We shall therefore omit a number of aspects that might interest a psychologist.

Chapter 9

REACTIONS OF THE BODY OF JESUS
UPON HIS SOUL

The humanity of Jesus is united substantially (hypostatically is the theologians' term) to His divinity in such a way as to form a single Person. But it would be a mistake to suppose a *Monophysite* union between His humanity and divinity, a kind of fusion, as if His human activities had been transformed and enjoyed divine omnipotence and impassibility. Jesus is perfect God and perfect man.

As man, Jesus has, just as we have, a body and a soul substantially united, though reacting one upon the other.

Here we have not to deal directly with His body; it is His soul which is the object of our contemplation. But the body reacts upon the soul, as we experience only too often, in pleasures and sorrows, attractions and aversions, changing moods, temptations to laziness and violence, to impurity and gluttony, and so on. These reactions are all caused or conditioned in us by the influence of our bodies. There is good reason, therefore, to consider the reactions of the body of Jesus on His soul.

The state of our bodies is influenced by the disorder of original sin and by the result of so many actual sins, our own and those of our ancestors back to our first father. In Jesus there was no sin, neither original nor actual, nor was there any tendency to sin. He was conceived virginally, in her in whom there was likewise no sin of any kind, in her who was all order and harmony.

Jesus, then, cannot serve as our direct model in our struggles against the temptations springing from our bodies, but in giving us His flesh to eat, He moderates our passions and gives us the strength to resist the most violent temptations. He gives us His own Immaculate Mother as our mother, whose very look and whose help in turn give us the sense of purity, an attraction for it, a strength, and a mastery over all our faculties.

Jesus had the physical forces necessary for His task, that is, for preaching, for apostolic journeys, for nights passed in prayer or in conversation with the timid who did not dare to come to Him by day, for fasts, and for lack of sleep.

His powers, however, were not unlimited: He needed help to carry His cross; He died after three hours on the cross though ordinarily the crucified remained alive for long hours, sometimes even for days; His two companions outlasted Him and to finish them off their legs had to be broken. It is true that they were not subjected to the same brutality as was Jesus; still Pilate was astonished that He should be already dead and asked the centurion for confirmation (Mk 5:42–45).

Jesus suffered like the rest of us. Many a time He used His miraculous power to cure the sick, twice to feed thousands of hungry listeners. He was never seen working a miracle to alleviate His own bodily needs or to dull the sharp pains inflicted upon Him. Without doubt His faculty of sensation was exceptionally refined, although completely subject to the control of the mind and the will. The more perfect a being is, the more perfect also is its capacity to suffer. This point must be kept in mind particularly in meditation on the Passion. But during His entire life, especially His public life, like other men, He had suffered hunger, thirst, fatigue, sleeplessness, and so on.

He had been hungry. The Evangelists mention His hunger after the fast of forty days (cf. Mt 4:1-11; Lk 4:1-13), and in connection with the barren fig tree (cf. Mk 11:12-14; Mt 21:19-22), because of the lessons to be drawn from these two incidents. But He had to suffer hunger on many other occasions and He depended on the charity of those whom He evangelized. Sometimes He was invited by the rich or He invited Himself, as at the house of Zacheus (cf. Lk 19:5), but that was not usual, much as He could have profited by it. If He had been alone, He could easily have found a welcome table, since hospitality in Palestine was generous. His constant companions were a group of twelve men in the flower of their age, and doubtless doors often remained closed to them. The incident of the Apostles passing through a wheat field on a Sabbath and rubbing the ears to eat the grain and still their hunger is only too clear (cf. Mt 12:1-8). Jesus lived the same kind of life as they. Often they had to content themselves with food bought with the alms which Judas managed, and, as John tells us, he was a thief.

Jesus suffered thirst. During His Passion, He complained of only one physical suffering, thirst (cf. Jn 19:28). It is true that He mentioned it to fulfill a prophecy, but it is likewise evident that the loss of so great a portion of His blood because of the scourging and the wounds of His hands and feet must have caused a burning thirst. During His wanderings throughout the summer, surely He suffered from thirst, and if He asked the Samaritan woman for a drink, when, exhausted from His journey, He sat on the rim of Jacob's well, He really was thirsty.

Jesus suffered from the heat. How often in summer He and His little band must have been tortured by the heat, as they passed from one town to another — always on foot — over rocky, dusty roads.

He suffered from cold. In Palestine, during the summer months, it is pleasant enough to sleep under the open sky, but in winter, when Jesus had to be content with any improvised shelter, His sleep must have been troubled many nights by the cold. To save men's souls He chose to be without lodging and to suffer all the resulting discomforts. One day, as He and His disciples trudged along, "a man said to him, 'I will follow thee wherever thou goest.' And Jesus said to him, 'The foxes have dens, and the birds of the air have nests, but the Son of Man has nowhere to lay his head.'" The man understood, for St. Luke does not add that he joined the group (Lk 9:57–58).

Jesus suffered fatigue. He preached from morning to night. Crowds followed Him and surrounded Him without allowing a moment's respite, not even for meals or for a bit of repose, and even at night Pharisees came for generous and patient explanations. At times, He was even overwhelmed. Crossing the lake one day, He was worn out to such a degree that He slept profoundly, even when a sudden storm struck, tossing the boat so violently that it was on the point of foundering. We recall Him at the gate of Sichar, tired, seated on the coping of the well of Jacob, the disciples sent off to the town to buy food. How touching to contemplate Him there, hungry and worn, still forgetting His hunger and fatigue, saving the soul of the sinful woman who had come out to fetch water. *Quaerens me sedisti lassus.*

Mary is also like us in all things except sin. Accordingly, like Jesus and like us, she had to suffer hunger, thirst, fatigue, and the inclemency of the weather. Because of her perfection, her sensitivity was very keen, like that of Jesus; harmoniously subject to mind and will, it intensified all her sufferings.

Holy Scripture makes no mention of any physical sufferings of Mary. Still, it is easy to imagine a certain number of them, particularly on her trip to Bethlehem and her stay there, on her

flight into Egypt, during her sojourn there, and on the return
trip. She was poor, because, at the Presentation of Jesus in the
temple and for her legal Purification, she presented two turtle-
doves, the offering of the poor. If she had been well off, she
would gladly have made the offering of the rich, a lamb and a
turtledove. Now, poverty entails all sorts of privation and suffering. However, she suffered with Jesus and for Him, and such
suffering was a joy to her.

Our Physical Suffering

All of us suffer in body — fatigue, insomnia, hunger, thirst —
just as Jesus did. Sometimes we are sick. The body of Jesus,
preserved from all the disorder caused by original sin, was not
subject to sickness. But during His Passion, He was tried by
tortures far more painful than any illness.

In our suffering, the thought that our pains are like those of
Jesus is a consolation and a comfort, and at the same time a way
of testifying our love for Him who willed to suffer incomparably
more for us in order to spare us eternal punishment. Jesus did
not have to suffer for Himself, He freely chose to suffer for us.
"He was offered because it was his own will" (Is 53:7). "Jesus
. . . for the joy set before him, endured a cross" (Heb 12:2). And
it was for love of me that He willed to suffer so much: "He
loved me and gave himself up for me" (Gal 2:20). How is it
possible not to accept sufferings for love of Him? That was the
thought that, through the ages, inspired so many Christians with
the courage to give even their lives for Christ.

Moreover, in return for the trials endured for Him, He
promises eternal happiness with Him and the Father. And my
sufferings, united to His, help Him save the souls of others.

The thought of Mary's happiness in sharing the trials and
sufferings of her Son for my salvation will make my acceptance
of sufferings with Jesus easier and more loving.

At prayer time, in meditation, or at Holy Communion, when
the body is fresh and disposed, it is relatively easy to speak to

our Lord. But when we are indisposed, tired out and sleepy, hungry, or thirsty, or, especially, when seriously sick, we feel incapable or unworthy of keeping company with Him. Did He not say: "Come to me, all you who labor and are burdened, and I will give you rest"? (Mt 11:28.) He understands us. What we feel, He has felt before us, and suffered from it as we do, and for us, in order precisely that we might go to Him in all confidence. "For we have not a high priest who cannot have compassion on our infirmities, but one tried as we are in all things except sin. Let us therefore draw near with confidence" (Heb 4:15-16). When we feel at ease during meditation or at Holy Communion, there is a certain consolation. When, however, we are out of sorts because of fatigue, sickness, or sleeplessness, and we go to Him confidently, telling Him that He was willing to suffer the same things and far worse, then there is consolation for Him. Let us have generosity enough to prefer His consolation to ours. At least we shall have the pleasure of knowing that we please Him.

Chapter 10

THE INTELLIGENCE OF JESUS

The humanity of Jesus possessed perfect intellectual powers, sense perception, memory, imagination, and reason, which enabled Him to acquire all kinds of natural knowledge. Parallel to these acquisitions was the knowledge of an infinity of supernatural realities. Theologians do not agree upon the scope of these latter, but it can be safely affirmed that Christ had the Beatific Vision from the first moment of His human existence, and He saw in God, whom He contemplated clearly and immediately with the eye of the spirit, the divine life in itself, and all things outside of God to the extent that this knowledge was necessary or useful for fulfilling His messianic mission. To impute to Him any ignorance or error in this area would be going counter to the clear text of Scripture which everywhere attests that Christ is the infallible Doctor of truth itself.[1]

We admire the natural intelligence of Jesus in the clarity with which He knows how to bring His teachings down to the level of humble and simple folks, through His charming and touching comparisons and parables. We also admire the finesse with which He answers the insidious questions of the hostile Pharisees, Sadducees, and Herodians, who sometimes went away astonished at His responses; at other times, so confounded that they dared not ask any more. Among these confutations, let us mention only the tribute to Caesar, the resurrection of the body, and Christ, the Son of David.

His supernatural knowledge manifests itself, above all, in the revelations about the life of God and the mystery of the Holy Trinity, and in His predictions of events, naturally unforeseeable, such as all the details of His Passion, His resurrec-

---

[1] Cf. the decree *Lamentabile*, prop. 34, 35; Denz. 2034, 2035.

tion on the third day, the denial of Peter, the flight of the Apostles, and the destruction of Jerusalem.

Other knowledge seems to be due at the same time to natural perspicacity and to supernatural enlightenment; for instance, the immediate knowledge of the characters of those who came to Him, the call of the first disciples (cf. Jn 1:35-51), the disposition of enthusiastic admirers (cf. Jn 2:25), of some Pharisees (cf. Lk 7:39-50; Mk 2:6-8; etc.), and His knowledge of Scripture (cf. Jn 7:15).

THE INTELLECT OF MARY. The intellectual faculties of Mary were also exceptional, befitting her vocation as Mother and educator of Christ, and cooperator with Him. But the soul of Mary did not enjoy the direct vision of God, since it was not hypostatically united to the divinity, as was that of her Son. In a way, however, she shared that vision, because she learned from Jesus mysteries hidden in God, meditating in her heart upon all that she saw in Him, or heard from Him or about Him (cf. Lk 2:19, 51). The Holy Spirit, who had descended upon her for the first time at her Immaculate Conception, and again with more light and love at the Incarnation, and then again on the day of Pentecost, made her understand the divine mysteries more and more fully.

Nevertheless, many things remained obscure to her. It was Mary, and not Jesus, who was to be our model for a life of faith and hope, and faith supposes difficulties mingled with clear insights. The natural penetration of her intellect, together with her humility, docility, and love, and the enlightenment granted by the Holy Spirit, made her advance always more and more into the depths of the Godhead, leaving at the same time enough mystery to make her faith heroic in the highest degree.[2]

OUR SUPERNATURAL KNOWLEDGE. In imitating Jesus in our knowledge of the divine mysteries we must follow Mary. We have received the gift of faith in baptism as she received it in her Immaculate Conception. Like her and united to her, we must listen to Jesus with a docile, humble, and loving heart, in-

---

[2] Cf. E. Neubert, S.M., *Mary in Doctrine*, pp. 204-206, on Mary's faith.

voking the Spirit of understanding, knowledge, wisdom, and counsel. Like her, we must meditate upon His teachings with our hearts. Like her, we must believe what God has revealed, despite the impenetrable obscurities of faith, in order to deserve to be proclaimed blessed, like her, for having believed. If, with these dispositions, under the guidance of Mary and of the Holy Spirit, we study the mysteries which Jesus taught us from His direct vision of the Father, we shall penetrate and live them far better than do the most subtle minds which trust in their own intellectual acumen. Limited though we be, like Mary, with the infallibility of Jesus, we shall share in all the divine truths and in all those especially which ought to guide our conduct, in proportion as we receive these teachings simply, humbly, and lovingly.

Chapter 11

THE WILL OF JESUS

The qualities of the will of Jesus stand out most clearly in His attitude toward the mission which He had received from His Father. (We shall study the object of this mission in the second part of this work.)

Jesus accomplished this mission with an unshakable will despite all obstacles:

Despite the wiles of Satan, who wished to turn Him from His mission by suggesting that He use His power to His own personal advantage (cf. Lk 4:1–13; Mt 4:1–11).

Despite the persistent efforts of His enemies, the Scribes, Pharisees, priests, and Sadducees, who came in crowds to heckle Him. He alone opposed them, for the Apostles did not know how to answer their objections as they themselves did not know too much about the teachings of Jesus. In all these exchanges, the enemies were worsted, and they despaired of ever getting the better of Him (cf. Mt 22:41–46).

Despite His fellow citizens of Nazareth, who were enthusiastic at first, but ended with trying to throw Him over the cliff on which the town was built (cf. Lk 4:16–30).

Despite the sympathetic crowds, who wished to make a king of Him, and then turned from Him because He persisted in having them accept the fact that they would have to eat His flesh and drink His blood. He permitted them to leave rather than explain to them that His flesh would be consecrated bread. He demanded the same of His dearest friends: "Do you also wish to go away?" (Jn 6:22–71.)

Despite His cousins who wanted to snatch Him from the

51

crowd and who, to succeed the more surely, brought His Mother
with them (cf. Mk 3:21, 31–35).

Despite His Apostles, who wanted to persuade Him not to
leave His solitude beyond the Jordan in order to place Himself
at the mercy of His enemies: "Rabbi, just now the Jews were
seeking to stone thee; and dost thou go there again?" (Jn 11:8.)

Despite Peter, whom He had just proclaimed blessed for having recognized His divinity, and who wished to turn Him from
His Passion: "Get behind me, satan, thou art a scandal to me;
for thou dost not mind the things of God, but those of men"
(Mt 16:22–23).

Despite the anguish which He caused His mother and St.
Joseph: "Did you not know that I must be about my Father's
business?" (Lk 2:49.) And later, the anguish which He caused
His Mother alone, by His bitter Passion.

His will is *direct*. He goes straight to the fulfillment of His
task. He never hesitates, never uses indirect means, never uses
subterfuges, nor compromises. His conduct is like His word:
Yes, yes; no, no. At times, He did withdraw from danger, at
Nazareth, for instance, and at Jerusalem (cf. Lk 4:30; Jn 10:31;
39–40). He withdrew into the region of Tyre and Sidon, into
the Decapolis, and to Perea, but that was because His hour,
the hour fixed by His Father, had not yet come. When His
hour came, He faced the danger without hesitation, in
Jerusalem.

On all occasions, He is Lord of the event. The strength of His
will appears above all in His Passion, which He foretold three
times.

The first prediction occurred after Peter's profession of faith
at Caesarea Philippi. Mark, the secretary of Peter, tells the story
in this way: "And he began to teach them that the Son of Man
must suffer many things, and be rejected by the elders and chief
priests and Scribes, and be put to death, and after three days

rise again." The Evangelist then makes the remark, which he had from Peter: "And what he said he spoke openly." Peter wanted to save Him from such a mistake, but the Master reproved him angrily: " 'Get behind me, satan, for thou dost not mind the things of God, but those of men.' And, calling the crowd together with his disciples, he said to them, 'If anyone wishes to come after me, let him deny himself, and take up his cross, and follow me' " (Mk 8:31–34).

Some time after that, journeying across Galilee, He again spoke to His disciples of His death and resurrection. "But," St. Mark comments, "they did not understand the saying, and were afraid to ask him" (Mk 9:30–31). They sensed that there was question of some tragedy that would befall the Master, but they found Him so set in His plans that they dared not approach Him on tho matter.

They had left Galilee, and crossed Samaria. "They were now on their way, going up to Jerusalem; and Jesus was walking on in front of them, and *they were in dismay, and those who followed were afraid.* And again taking the Twelve, he began to tell them what would happen to him," foretelling for the third time His coming Passion and death (cf. Mk 10:32–34).

The group then arrived at Jerusalem. Jesus raised Lazarus from the dead and went up to the temple in triumph, although He knew that in five days the crowd, which now acclaimed Him, would cry out, "Crucify Him!"

His courage showed particularly in His Passion. In the Garden of Olives, He freely presented Himself to the band led by Judas; with a word, He threw to the ground those who had come to take Him, healed the ear of one of them, protected His disciples, taunted His enemies for the treachery and stupidity with which they came to capture Him, and then allowed Himself to be bound and led away, because His hour of darkness had come.

In the presence of the high priest, He disdained to justify Himself, a matter that would have been quite simple against self-contradicting witnesses. He replied only to affirm that He

was the Messias and God, and to announce that He would come
as supreme judge upon the clouds of heaven.

He refused even to clear Himself before Pilate. It would have
been easy for Jesus to encourage Pilate to resist the Jewish accusers, because the governor was ill-disposed toward them already and shaken by a religious scruple, but Jesus would have
none of it.

Herod would have been gratified to see Jesus work a miracle,
and without doubt would have sent him back acquitted, but
Jesus did not deign to give him a single word.

He was scourged, crowned with thorns, compelled to carry
His cross, finally nailed to it; but, at every moment, He remained noble to such a degree that one of the thieves recognized His divinity, and the centurion confessed to those
about him, "Truly this man was the Son of God" (Mt 15:39).

From where did Jesus draw this strength and firmness of
will? From His perfect nature, which was equal to His mission.
From His clear vision of what He wanted. From the fact that
He wished only and completely the will of His Father. From
the help of a special grace which He had long and urgently demanded in the Garden of Olives.

THE WILL OF MARY. Mary will make us understand better and
imitate the strength of the will of Jesus. All her life she was the
"strong woman."

She needed strength of will in the presence of Gabriel to accept (and so simply) an almost infinite responsibility, on which
depended the future of earth and even of heaven; also, to keep
silent when her pregnancy threw Joseph into such anguished
doubts; and not to complain of the lack of welcome for Jesus at
Bethlehem; as well as not to be frightened by the perspectives
hinted at by the old priest Simeon; and not to protest the orders
to flee from Herod.

She needed strength, too, to endure the agony of that un-
explainable disappearance of the Child Jesus in Jerusalem; to
live for thirty years at the side of her Son, to watch Him grow
in stature, in wisdom, and in grace, and to sense every day that

the hour was drawing nearer when He would be a "sign of contradiction" to His people, and when the sword would pierce her own heart.

She needed strength particularly to assist at His Passion, and to follow Him up Calvary, when even His Apostles hid themselves; and to stand up bravely at the foot of the cross to see Him expire before her eyes.

And she never complained, never dreamed of escaping any trial. At the announcement of His Passion, she did not cry out like Peter: "God forbid! That will never happen." Standing before Jesus nailed to the cross, she did not ask of heaven what had become of the promises of Gabriel that her Son would sit on the throne of David and reign forever.

There was never a hero or a martyr with the courage of Mary, a simple and sweet virgin. The strength of her will was drawn from sources similar to those which Jesus used: the perfection of her nature, never weakened by either original or actual sin; perfect fidelity to God's will, from her Immaculate Conception to her death. Her reply to Gabriel, "Behold the handmaid of the Lord; be it done to me according to thy word," expresses her attitude at every moment of her life. The consideration of the courage of her Son also sustained her own courage, as did the joy of suffering for Him, and with Him, for the glory of the Father and the redemption of all men, who were His brothers and her children.

OUR WILLS. Our wills are weak, capricious, changeable. Jesus and Mary will teach us to make them strong and steady.

Our wills are weak partly because of our nature, wounded by original sin and by our own actual sins. Meditation on the unshakable wills of Jesus and Mary, together with the graces which they will obtain for us if we ask for them, will give us a heroic will power such as that of the martyrs. The thought of St. Paul bears meditation: "For when I am weak, then I am strong" (2 Cor 12:10).

Our wills are also weak and inconstant, because often we do not know what we want. Then it is not reason that guides us, but caprice, a whim of the moment, a silly satisfaction, or the example of others. And since all that changes from moment to moment, we are incapable of perseverance. The wills of Jesus and Mary were determined by the will of God. If, before making up our minds on anything at all, especially on a matter of importance, we demanded of God, or of Mary, their will or their preference, we too would be able to achieve constancy. Our love for Jesus, Mary, and souls will give us the courage to do what, without these motives, would surpass our capability. The more intimate our union with our Lord and His Mother, the stronger shall our wills be, not with a wild energy, but with both smoothness and strength, like those of Christ and our Mother.

Chapter 12

THE FEARS OF JESUS

If Jesus always gave proof of steadfast courage, there was, nevertheless, a moment in His life when He knew fear. Five days before His death, the day of His triumphal entry into Jerusalem, He said: "The hour has come for the Son of Man to be glorified. Amen, Amen, I say to you, unless the grain of wheat falls into the ground and dies, it remains alone. But if it dies, it brings forth much fruit. . . ." Then He added suddenly, "Now my soul is troubled. And what shall I say? Father save me from this hour!" Then He recovered His poise: "No, this is why I came to this hour. Father, glorify thy name" (Jn 12:23–28). The glory of His Father had to win out over fear.

In fact, from the first moment of His existence, the glory of the Father was His final goal. According to the Epistle to the Hebrews, "Coming into the world, he says, 'Sacrifice and oblation thou wouldst not, but a body thou hast fitted to me. . . . Then said I, "Behold, I come . . . to do thy will, O God'" (Heb 10:5–7).

All His life that objective was before Him. We saw above, that on three different occasions He foretold His Passion to His Apostles, and He mentioned how important suffering was to Him, and that on the third occasion Mark related, "They were now on their way, going up to Jerusalem; and Jesus was walking on in front of them." It was He who had to suffer, so He walked at the head. "They were in dismay, and those who followed were afraid. And again taking the Twelve, he began to tell them what would happen to him" (Mk 10:32).

And yet, so firm and resolute had He showed Himself that

the nearer the fateful hour approached, the more He felt the horror of what awaited Him.

"I have come to cast fire upon the earth, and what will I but that it be kindled?" He said on Palm Sunday. "But I have a baptism to be baptized with [that is, to be plunged into a bath of suffering] and how distressed I am until it is accomplished" (Lk 12:50).

Now, here is how He was going to be plunged in it. St. Mark reports: "And they came to a country place called Gethsemani, and he said to his disciples, 'Sit down here, while I pray.' And he took with him Peter and James and John and he began to feel dread and to be exceedingly troubled. And he said to them, 'My soul is sad, even unto death. Wait here and watch.' And going forward a little, he fell on the ground, and began to pray that, if it were possible, the hour might pass from him; and he said, 'Abba, Father, all things are possible to thee. Remove this cup from me'" (Mk 14:32–36).

For thirty-three years He had prepared Himself for this hour, and now He asked that it pass far from Him! Shortly before, when Peter wanted to dissuade Him from His Passion, He told him indignantly, "Get behind me, satan!" and here He Himself wished to turn away from it. Just a while ago, when they left the supper room for Gethsemani, He said: "The prince of the world is coming, and in me he has nothing. But he comes that the world may know that I love the Father, and that I do as the Father has commanded me. Arise, let us go from here" (Jn 14:30–31). Still He would like to change the order of His Father; fulfilling it was to show the world His love for Him.

Up to this moment, all His life, He confronted His enemies and every danger with a calm courage, and He was going to show that same serene, noble courage before the Great Council, before Pilate and Herod, during the scourging, the crowning with thorns, and the three hours of agony upon the cross. Why, then, those terrible fears in the Garden that made Him sweat blood, why those cries of anguish to His Father?

First of all, because He was a man just as we are, like us in

everything except sin. Now it is perfectly human to be seized
with fear in face of a great danger, especially one that is horrible,
imminent, and positively unavoidable. The human nature of
Jesus, with a particularly delicate sensitivity, recoiled from all
the torments which He saw breaking upon Him: the scourging,
the crowning with thorns, the carrying of the cross, the cruci-
fixion, and the slow agony on the cross. With this physical tor-
ment there was mingled the vision of other sufferings, even more
terrible, to which we shall return, the sins that weighed upon
Him, the ingratitude of men, the futility for so many souls of
all these torments and even of His death. His human nature
trembled and recoiled with horror and begged the Father to
spare Him that trial.

Of course there were other reasons why the soul of Jesus was
harassed by such fears. Among them were these:

To expiate the countless sins of weakness and cowardice, committed by men, big men and small men.

To teach us how to act when nature cringes before a trial that
seems beyond our powers, and, like Jesus, to demand of the
Father, in the name of the fears of Jesus, that He either remove
the trial, if it be His good pleasure, or give us the strength to do
His holy will, if the trial must persist.

To convince us of the reality of His sufferings, because, without the revelation of His agony, without seeing Him endure all
the torments of His Passion with such a firm and noble courage,
would we not be tempted to tell ourselves that His divinity must
have suppressed or at least diminished the acuteness of His
sufferings? Without those fears of Jesus, His Passion would touch
us less, and we would not sense so vividly His infinite love for us.

THE FEARS OF MARY. Was there not an agony for Mary as
there had been for Jesus, when her courage was proved by a
mortal fear, just as that of Jesus was? The Gospels do not mention it, but do they not permit us to suppose a fear of this sort?
Not only do the Gospels recount the sorrows of Mary, all due
to her bonds with Jesus, namely, the perplexities of Joseph,
Bethlehem, Egypt, the Temple of Jerusalem, and Calvary, but

they mention expressly the prophecy of Simeon, telling her of the sword which should pierce her heart because of her Son. Moreover, we see Jesus sharing His mysteries, His functions, His prerogatives with His Mother. Did He not also wish to share with her, who was His associate in our redemption, the anguish of His Passion? He knew that she would be most grateful for it. We may also suppose that there were hours of suspense, when she was seized by the fear of what awaited her Son, and when she prayed: "Father, if it is possible, remove this chalice from my Jesus! Still, Thy will be done not mine." And yet, like the will of Jesus, Mary's did not flinch one instant.

Particularly in contemplating the agony of Jesus, it is important to gain entrance into His soul through Mary. We are, perhaps, more easily touched by the anguish of a woman, of a mother, than we are by that of a man, even of a Man-God, and the griefs of the Mater Dolorosa help us feel more keenly those of her Son. *Fac me tecum pie flere, crucifixo condolere donec ego vixero!* "Let me mingle tears with thee, mourning Him who mourned for me, all the days that I may live."

OUR FEARS. In our moments of enthusiasm, such as solemn Communion, retreat, a religious or mission congress, religious profession or ordination, we are ready to suffer anything rather than offend our Lord, to give ourselves without reserve for a holy cause. But when the hour for sacrifice strikes, when we sense only our weakness, in times of sickness or of physical and moral depression, in moments of disgust at any trial, we fear, we hesitate, our fighting spirit has vanished. What is to be done?

At such moments can we still present ourselves to our Lord? We feel so uninspired, so timid, so different from what we were when we swore eternal loyalty to Him. How present ourselves, then, before Him?

We must do it in all humility but in utter confidence. "For we have not a high priest who cannot have compassion on our infirmities, but one tried as we are in all things" (Heb 4:15). Let us go to Him. He will not say to us: "What? You swore that you were ready for everything, even to die for Me, and now, faced with the little sacrifice that I ask of you, frightened, you turn away; where is your courage? What has happened to your promises?" No; He understands us and can sympathize with us. He will tell us to continue to pray, as He did in the Garden, and, despite all, to wish only God's holy will. He will send an angel, or, even better, His Mother, the Mother of Sorrows, to teach us to suffer as He did, with Him and for Him, and she will pass on her courage, a courage more humble but also more firm.

Chapter 13

THE JOYS OF JESUS

THE SENSITIVITY OF JESUS. Whenever there was question of the mission He had received from His Father, Jesus displayed a will power that was unshakable, unyielding, and most adamant, even for those who were dearest to Him. But, on the other hand, when His Father's mission was not at stake, He showed Himself full of feeling, and as tender and delicate as the most perfect heart of a woman, for He received His humanity solely from a woman, from the tenderest and the strongest woman who ever lived.

We shall have occasion later on to admire these delicate variations when we meditate on how He fulfilled His mission toward His father and toward men. Here we shall contemplate His joys and His sorrows.

The greatest and the most enduring joys of Jesus came to Him from His Father. They were the following:

First, the joy of the Beatific Vision, from the moment of His conception, of which we shall be able to form an idea, only when we share it with Him in heaven; then, the joy of always doing the will of His Father, which assured Him profound and continual peace and happiness, even amid the sorrows of His missionary life and of His Passion; the joy of offering to the heavenly Father a sacrifice worthy of Him; the joy of reconciling heaven and earth; the joy of making the Father known, loved, and served, and of changing His enemies into loving children, who would people heaven.

Second, there were the joys that came to Him from the men to whom He had been sent, particularly from the souls who best understood Him, who gave themselves most generously to Him, humble, simple, honest souls, detached from earthly goods and consecrated entirely to God.

During His hidden life, He lived with Mary and Joseph. He spoke to them about the Father, about the kingdom of heaven, about poverty, simplicity, and love for God and for men. He would never again be understood as He was by those dear ones. What unsurpassable joy, that long intimacy at Nazareth, for Jesus, Mary, and Joseph!

The beginnings of His ministry in Galilee brought Him other joys. The crowds which followed Him enthusiastically were, for the most part, simple, poor, believing, religious folks. And it was with enthusiasm that He addressed those beatific words to them:

"Blessed are you poor, for yours is the kingdom of God. Blessed are you who hunger now, for you shall be satisfied. Blessed are you who weep now, for you shall laugh. Blessed shall you be when men hate you, and when they shut you out, and reproach you, and reject your name as evil, because of the Son of Man. Rejoice on that day and exult, for behold your reward is great in heaven. For in the selfsame manner their fathers used to treat the prophets" (Lk 6:20–23). According to his method, Matthew gave a general scope to these words: "Blessed are the poor in spirit. . . . Blessed are they who mourn . . ." (Mt 5:3–10).

The seventy-two sent out on the mission "returned with joy, saying, 'Lord, even the devils are subject to us in thy name.' But he said to them, '. . . Do not rejoice in this, that the spirits are subject to you; but rejoice in this, that your names are written in heaven.'" St. Luke adds: "In that very hour Jesus rejoiced in the Holy Spirit and said, 'I praise thee, Father, Lord of heaven and earth, that thou didst hide these things from the wise and prudent, and didst reveal them to little ones. Yes, Father, for such was thy good pleasure'" (Lk 10:17–21). Then, thinking of the happiness of these simple men who recognized the Messias, He turned and said to them privately: "Blessed are the eyes

that see what you see! For I say to you, many prophets and
kings have desired to see what you see, and they have not seen
it, and to hear what you hear, and they have not heard it"
(Lk 10:23–24).

Neither was the joy of Jesus less, when He heard Peter acknowledge Him as the Messias, the very Son of God. "Then Jesus
answered and said, 'Blessed art thou, Simon Bar-Jona, for flesh
and blood has not revealed this to thee, but my Father in heaven.
And I say to thee, thou art Peter, and upon this rock I will build
my Church, and the gates of hell shall not prevail against it.
And I will give thee the keys of the kingdom of heaven; and
whatever thou shalt bind on earth shall be bound in heaven,
and whatever thou shalt loose on earth shall be loosed in
heaven'" (Mt 16:13–20).

He permits us to conjecture what joy the generosity and sincerity of the Apostles caused Him, despite all their faults and
earthly views. Peter said to Him once: "Behold, we have left all
and followed thee; what then shall we have?" And Jesus said
to them, "Amen I say to you that you who have followed me,
in the regeneration when the Son of Man shall sit on the throne
of his glory, shall also sit on twelve thrones, judging the twelve
tribes of Israel" (Mt 19:27–28). And later, in the Cenacle, after
the institution of the Eucharist, He said: "You are they who have
continued with me in my trials. And I appoint to you a kingdom,
even as my Father has appointed to me" (Lk 22:28).

Joy again filled Him when He heard the centurion say: "Lord,
I am not worthy that thou shouldst come under my roof; but
only say the word, and my servant will be healed. For I too
am a man subject to authority, and have soldiers subject to me:
and I say to one, 'Go,' and he goes; and to another, 'Come,' and
he comes; and to my servant, 'Do this,' and he does it." And
when Jesus heard this, He marveled, and said to those who were
following Him, "Amen I say to you, I have not found such great
faith in Israel" (Mt 8:8–10).

The same thing happened in answer to the faith and humility
of the woman of Canaan who had begged Him to cure her

daughter possessed by a devil. Jesus said to her: "O woman, great is thy faith! Let it be done to thee as thou wilt" (Mt 15:28).

What a joy also for Him to bless the little children (cf. Mk 10:14), or to meet the rich young man who had observed all the precepts since his youth! About the latter Mark relates: "And Jesus, looking upon him, loved him" (Mk 10:21).

All the sinners, men and women, who simply acknowledged their faults and tried to love Him all the more for having offended Him more, caused Him great happiness. He showed it in His most touching parables: that of the lost sheep which was returned by the shepherd, that of the lost drachma found by the housekeeper, and, above all, that of the prodigal son (Lk 15:4–31). He showed it in His very conduct. He enjoyed inviting Himself to the house of Zacchaeus because the man was sincerely religious and was ready to make fourfold restitution for all his cheating (Lk 19:1–10). You sense that He was happy in the company of Martha of Bethany, and, even more so, in that of her sister, Mary, the notorious sinner of Magdala, who testified her love with such humility and such warmth (cf. Lk 10:38–42). And do you not feel a note of joy in His reply to the humble, trustful thief on the cross: "Amen I say to thee, this day thou shalt be with me in paradise"? (Lk 23:43.)

He experienced joy even in contemplating dumb animals because they, too, are creatures of the Father and objects of His providence. Ravens neither sow nor reap, still God feeds them. Not one of the sparrows will fall from the housetop without the Father's leave (cf. Mt 10:29). He observed with joy the birds of the air which pilfer the seeds falling by the wayside (cf. Mt 13:4), the chicks which the hen gathers under her wings (cf. Mt 13:37), the lost sheep which the happy shepherd carries back on his shoulders (cf. Lk 15:5), and even the lilies of the field which are more splendid than Solomon in all his glory (cf. Mt 6:28).

Chapter 14

THE JOYS OF MARY

To Mary, just as to Jesus, unspeakable joys were caused by her relations with God. Among them were the following:

The joys of her Immaculate Conception, which according to a probable opinion, were even conscious.[1] To know God from the first moment of her existence; to perceive herself so deeply loved by Him; herself so pure, so beautiful, so freely overwhelmed with marks of His goodness, so capable of returning love without measure for His infinite love with an ever increasing intensity, and so unconditionally and completely consecrated to Him — what reasons for joy!

The joy of discovering later, when she knew other men with their defects and their sins, that God had sheltered her from every fault and even from every inclination to evil.

The joy of consecrating her virginity to Him, to be His without a rival.

The joy of finding in Joseph a spouse who understood, respected, and accepted her decision of virginity and perfect purity.

The joys, too, of the Annunciation which she sang in her *Magnificat*.

The joy of being an instrument of her Son in sanctifying His precursor and of filling her old cousin Elizabeth with a prophetic spirit.

Then the unspeakable joys of her relations to Him whom she carried in her womb, and whom she was to give to the world; her share even in the joys of Jesus, for she existed only for Jesus, and had the same interests and loves as He. Since Jesus

---

[1] Cf. E. Neubert, S.M., *Mary in Doctrine*, pp. 162–165.

had received all His humanity from her alone, they were both, even physiologically, predisposed to rejoice and be grieved similarly and for the same reasons.

There were, first of all, those intimate joys of the hidden life. As Jesus took deep pleasure in merely looking at His Mother, in speaking with her, in carrying out her wishes, in foreseeing and doing every imaginable thing to please her, so also Mary found similar pleasure in meeting her Son's gaze, in receiving marks of affection or unexpected attentions from Him, in observing His satisfaction at her readiness to give her all for the success of His plans.

Her role as mother of the Messias was to make of her a mother of sorrows; but each one of these sorrows caused her a pleasure, bitter and yet sweeter than any other consolation, that of being able to suffer for Him.

The awful prophecy of Simeon, whose fulfillment came closer each day, brought its own special joy, that of seeing her Son glorify the Father by the sacrifice of Himself, and thus bring back a host of loving children to share for all eternity the beatitude of that same Father, of the Son, and of the Holy Spirit.

Then, during the public life of Jesus, there was the pleasure of sharing the joys of her Son in His contacts with humble, simple, unselfish souls, who were so full of faith. There were sinners, too, who after their conversion, became among the most fervent of His disciples. St. John mentions Mary Magdalen as present on Calvary, at the foot of the cross of Jesus, at the side of His Mother. The purest of virgins next to a former public sinner, possessed by seven devils! There is not the least doubt that the Blessed Virgin shared the affection of Jesus for that generous convert.

Then the hour of the Passion struck, the hour foretold, long ago, by Simeon, and ever since then, present so often to the mind and heart of Mary; the hour when her Son had to be, for the entire nation, a subject of contradiction, the cause of the fall and resurrection of a great multitude, and when her own soul had to be pierced with a sword. Poor Mother!

Even at that hour, she experienced a sweet joy which she would never have exchanged for other consolations, that of being again near her Son after nearly three years of separation, and precisely at the moment of His supreme sacrifice, in such a way that in her heart she could share His Passion.

Still another joy, even more intense, supported her in her martyrdom, the thought of the happy effects which this Passion gave her, namely, that the Father was to be glorified and the human race to be redeemed. St. Pius X brought out this fact in his encyclical of February 2, 1904, in which he defined the role of the Blessed Virgin toward all humanity. "When the supreme hour arrived for Jesus, the Blessed Virgin was seen standing at the foot of the cross, no doubt transfixed by the horror of the spectacle, and still happy because her Son was immolating Himself for the salvation of mankind."

She understood that Jesus had wished her to be near Him at that hour, as formerly she had been near when He blessed His precursor enclosed in the womb of Elizabeth, and when He manifested Himself to Jews and Gentiles in the person of the shepherds and the Magi. It was by the union of her will and sufferings with the will and sufferings of her Son that she should collaborate with Him for the glory of the Father and for the salvation of men, whom she would bring forth in great pain. And, without doubt, to make her understand better her maternal mission, and in that solemn moment to proclaim it to the universe, Jesus said to her, "Woman, behold thy son," and to John, "Behold thy mother." At that moment she had the consolation of giving birth by a new life, by the very life of her Son, to the countless multitude of men, occupied solely, just then, with the things of this world, actually putting to death her only Son by their sins.

Already at that hour she glimpsed that marvelous transformation. She heard Jesus pray, "Father, forgive them, for they do not know what they are doing." And the Mother joined her supplication with that of her Son. Then, one of the two malefactors crucified with Jesus, who had just blasphemed Him, suddenly said: "Lord, remember me when thou comest into thy kingdom." And Jesus said to him, "Amen, I say to thee, this day thou shalt be with me in paradise." Luke, the Evangelist of the Blessed Virgin, is the only one who reports these words to us (23:42–43).

Doubtless, a fierce anguish then choked the heart of Mary when she heard her Son cry out: "My God, my God, why hast thou forsaken me?" (Mk 15:34.) But she recalled that they are the first words of a psalm, the twenty-first, which foretells the Passion, but which terminates in a cry of victory. In fact, soon she heard Jesus say: "Father, into thy hands I commend my spirit." It is again St. Luke who brings us this word. And then Mary saw the bystanders strike their breasts and she heard the centurion confess, "Truly this man was the Son of God" (Mk 15:39; Lk 23:45).

Three days after, she saw her Son again, beautiful, glorious, and happy beyond words. What a delight after all those torments! Without doubt, she saw Him several times. Perhaps He still had instructions for her, as He had for the Apostles, in view of her role as mother of the newborn Church. The Evangelists do not speak of this, no more than they speak of their conversations through thirty years of hidden life. They were Mary's secrets, and for her alone.

Forty days later she saw her Son ascend into heaven to sit at the right hand of the Father. It was separation for her, but a joy ineffable, nonetheless, for she existed only for that Son, and she was happy when He was happy.

Chapter 15

OUR JOYS AS CHRISTIANS

Jesus desires His disciples to live joyfully. In the Old Testament, the psalms and the prophets announced His coming as a tremendously joyous event (cf. Ps 71:109; Is 54:1, 5; Jl 1:18, 21, 23; Za 9:4, 10; So 3:14–17).

The first word of Gabriel to Mary was an exhortation to joy: "Be glad, you who are full of grace" (Lk 1:26; that is the translation of the Greek word *khaire* which St. Luke used. It is the meaning which the Greek Fathers gave to the word, and which the Messianic promises, just mentioned, suggest). And the angel — Gabriel, again, without doubt, because he is the angel of the Incarnation — began with saying to the shepherds of Bethlehem: "Do not be afraid, for behold, I bring you news of great joy which shall be to all the people" (Lk 2:10).

The first instructions of Jesus to the crowds were proclamations of joy for His disciples: "Blessed are you poor. . . . Blessed are you who hunger now. . . . Blessed are you who weep now. . . . Blessed shall you be when men hate. . . . Rejoice . . . and exult" (Lk 6:20–22).

He wished His presence among His disciples to be one long feast and He dispensed them from fasting during it. One day the disciples of John approached Him and asked: "Why do we and the Pharisees often fast, whereas thy disciples do not fast?" And Jesus said to them, "Can the wedding guests mourn as long as the bridegroom is with them? But the days will come when the bridegroom shall be taken away from them, and then they will fast" (Mt 9:14 ff).

He demanded that His disciples preserve that inner joy, even when He should no longer be with them. At the discourse after the Last Supper, when He announced that the moment had come for Him to be delivered to His enemies and to be crucified, He insisted that they remain full of joy. "As the Father has loved me, I also have loved you. Abide in my love. . . . These things I have spoken to you that my joy may be in you and that your joy may be made full" (Jn 15:9–11).

When He told them that He would have to leave, sadness overcame them. Consoling them with the promise of a new joy, one that would not be taken away from them, He said: "Amen, amen, I say to you, that you shall weep and lament, but the world shall rejoice; and you shall be sorrowful, but your sorrow shall be turned into joy. A woman about to give birth has sorrow, because her hour has come. But when she has brought forth the child, she no longer remembers the anguish for her joy that a man is born into the world. And you therefore have sorrow now; but I will see you again, and your heart shall rejoice, and your joy no one shall take from you" (Jn 16:20–22).

Then He prayed to the Father for His disciples with the prayer called "sacerdotal": "While I was with them, I kept them in thy name. . . . But now I am coming to thee; and these things I speak in the world, *in order that they may have my joy* made full in themselves" (Jn 17:12 ff.).

Like their Master, the Apostles taught a doctrine of joy. St. Paul, especially in his Epistles, comes back at least fifty times upon the duty of joy. To the Romans he wished, "peace and joy in the Holy Spirit" (Rom 14:17); "May the God of hope fill you with all joy and peace" (Rom 15:13). To the Philippians he recommended very clearly, "Rejoice in the Lord always; again I say, rejoice" (Phil 4:4). The Gospel is *good news,* the news of joy, not of a gloomy, depressing pessimism.

Why should we be glad? First of all, because of the joys of Jesus and Mary. We are not egoists. If we are true Christians, our great joy is everything that ever pleased and still pleases

Jesus and Mary. Contemplating their joys, we make them ours. We do that, not by a process of reasoning but by a supernatural sympathy which will make the noble dispositions which we see in their hearts pass into ours. If we read the life of an historical character, his joys may touch us only slightly. But if we learn of the joys of a person who is very near and dear to us, we naturally rejoice with him. Now Jesus and Mary are not merely historical persons; they are alive, and near to us; they hear and see us; they love us and are preoccupied with us. In reviewing their joys, enumerated above, we must put ourselves in their loving presence, and enjoy every moment with them.

Besides their joys, which we can divine in the Gospels, they have others that are actual: the victories of the Church; the saintliness of many of her members; the success of her missionaries and other apostles; the heroism of her martyrs; the good realized by us and by the group of which we form a part; the good done by other members of the Church, particularly by those who have done what we could not do. In all this, there is question, not of our glory, but of the glory of God and of His Church.

Every Christian is also happy because of the countless graces which he has received and is now receiving: to be another Christ, sharing in the divine life; to be a well-beloved child of Mary as Jesus was; to possess the peace which God gives to whoever does His will; perhaps to be called to a particular vocation, the object of a very special love of God.

Then there is the joy of making our Lord and His Mother known and loved. There is the intense joy of converting a sinner, or of discovering and forming an elite soul.

There are joys in suffering for the cause of Jesus, of Mary, and of others. In them we can say with St. Paul: "I am filled with comfort, I overflow with joy in all our troubles" (2 Cor 7:4).

There are joys even in our weaknesses and faults, when we give Jesus a triple joy, "going to Him with His Mother, with our misery and our confidence,"[1] and the joy of giving a triple joy

---

[1] Cf. Neubert, *Life of Union With Mary*, pp. 82–83.

to Mary in begging her to lead us to Jesus, to tell Him our misery and our confidence.

There are, unbelievable as they seem, joys even in our failures; if we offer them to God and unite them with the failures of Jesus in His Passion, they prepare triumphs for the interests of Jesus.

Of course there are false joys, which are forbidden. We are not permitted to satisfy our fallen nature by committing sin, or to enjoy the evils that befall an enemy or a rival. They are false inasmuch as they make us unhappy, and take from the soul that peace of God which surpasses all understanding. Forbidding oneself these false joys brings true joy, the joy which Jesus promised to His disciples and which no one can take from them.

Every Christian who lives his religion has a taste of true joy. A gloomy Christian does not think and feel like a Christian; he thinks and feels like the egoist that he is.

Chapter 16

THE SORROWS OF JESUS

If Jesus tasted profound joys, His sorrows were no less profound — and far more frequent.

In contemplating the sorrows of Jesus, it must be remembered that, since sorrow results from unrequited or resisted love, and since His love for His Father, His Mother, and for all men, His brothers, surpasses all our understanding, so also His sorrows are beyond all imagination.

Even at Nazareth, in the company of Mary and Joseph, Jesus suffered their pains, caused by the difficulties of mere existence, but, above all, those caused by Himself, as, when at the age of twelve, to obey His heavenly Father, He plunged them into agonizing grief, and when many a time He saw the face of His Mother cloud as she recalled the prophecy of Simeon.

Among the inhabitants of Nazareth, besides the simple and religious folk, He had to deal with others who were solely preoccupied with their material interests, rendering His Father only an external cult, some of them concealing revolting vices under the false front of service of God and scrupulous observance of the law.

During His public life, we see Him at times saddened by the misfortunes which befell those whom He loved, with a sorrow that was heightened because of the exquisite delicacy of His love. He wept over His friend Lazarus. After having retired across the Jordan, because of His enemies, he returned to Bethany where Lazarus had just died. There He found Martha disconsolate. He tried to console her with thoughts on the resurrection. Martha went to call her sister, Mary. "When, therefore, Mary came where Jesus was, and saw him, she fell at his feet, and said to him, 'Lord, if thou hadst been here, my brother would not have died.' When, therefore, Jesus saw her weeping, and the Jews who had come with her weeping, he groaned in spirit and was troubled, and said, 'Where have you laid him?' They said to him, 'Lord, come and see.' And Jesus wept." ("And Jesus wept." This is perhaps the shortest and most touching verse in all Sacred Scripture.) "The Jews therefore said, 'See how he loved him.' . . . Jesus therefore, again groaning in himself, came to the tomb . . . and cried out with a loud voice, 'Lazarus, come forth!' And at once he who had been dead came forth" (Jn 11:32–44).

Jesus also wept over Jerusalem. The very day of His triumph, Palm Sunday, "when he drew near and saw the city, he wept over it saying, 'If thou hadst known, in this thy day, even thou, the things that are for thy peace! But now they are hidden from thy eyes. For days will come upon thee when thy enemies will throw up a rampart about thee, and surround thee and shut thee in on every side, and will dash thee to the ground and thy children within thee, and will not leave in thee one stone upon another, because thou hast not known the time of thy visitation'" (Lk 19:41–44).

Jesus had to endure the sorrows, more persistent and overwhelming, caused by the men He had come to save. It is true that the crowds usually followed Him with enthusiasm, especially at the beginning of His preaching, but they were attracted by the novelty of His doctrine, His miracles for their benefit, and because of their Messianic hopes. In reality, they did not understand Him. They could not understand the idea of a Messias who would not drive out the Romans, and would not change their own lot, material and political. Sometimes they acclaimed Him and tried to make Him their king; sometimes they withdrew from Him, saying, "Who can understand His demands?" Then again they cried out, "Hosanna to the Son of David!" and five days after, "Crucify Him!"

Jesus had the right to count more on those who knew Him best. The townspeople of Nazareth had seen Him during thirty years and had been edified by His life and that of His parents. When He returned to preach to them, at first they were charmed by the words of grace that fell from His lips. Then jealousy turned them against Him and they tried to throw Him from the steep cliff on which the town was built. "And he could not work any miracle there, beyond curing a few sick people by laying his hands upon them." And St. Mark adds, "And he marveled because of their unbelief" (Mk 6:1–5; Lk 4:22–30).

A young man came to Him to ask what he had to do to gain eternal life. He was a youth who had kept all the commandments since his boyhood, and Mark observes that Jesus "looking upon him, loved him." However, He was disappointed in that choice young soul (cf. Mk 10:17–22).

Even the Apostles of Jesus did not understand Him most of the time, as they clung so tightly to their worldly dreams. The leader among them, Peter, even wished to deter Him from His mission. On the eve of His Passion, after He had just spoken to them of His approaching sufferings, they disputed among themselves about who was the greatest. When Jesus announced that He was to be arrested and put to death, all of them protested that they would follow Him even to death. Two hours later they all abandoned Him.

Judas, more than any other Apostle, broke the heart of Jesus. For more than a year, since the episode in the synagogue of Capharnaum, the Master had foretold his treachery in veiled terms. When a large number of the disciples deserted, Jesus turned to the Twelve and asked: "Do you also wish to go away?" Simon Peter therefore answered, "Lord to whom shall we go? Thou hast the words of everlasting life, and we have come to believe and to know that thou art the Christ, the Son of God." Jesus was pleased with Peter's answer, but the loyalty of the little band made Him sense all the more sorrowfully the future betrayal of Judas. "Have I not chosen you, the Twelve? Yet one of you is a devil."

During all that year, Jesus saw Judas at His side and bore up with him patiently, to try to bring him around; Judas even remained treasurer of the group. The poor man became more obstinate in his evil dispositions, believing, perhaps, that Jesus suspected nothing.

At the Last Supper, the presence of Judas was insupportable. Jesus, in His farewell to the disciples, gave them His flesh to eat, and His blood to drink, and made them the leaders of the Church which He was about to establish. John sensed that He was ill at ease and remarked: "He was troubled in spirit, and said solemnly, 'Amen, amen, I say to you, one of you will betray me.'" Not a single one understood. Jesus offered a portion of the dipped bread to Judas saying, "What thou dost, do quickly." And the traitor left the room. Relieved, Jesus continued: "Now is the Son of Man glorified, and God is glorified in him. . . . Little children, yet a little while I am with you." Then followed those tender words after the supper and His sacerdotal prayer (cf. John 13 and 14).

A sorrow, far more human, was to come over Jesus in the garden of Gethsemani. We mentioned it before in treating of the fears of Jesus. But this fear was accompanied by a sorrow, so depressing, that He said to His three intimates: "My soul is sad, even unto death. Wait here and watch" (Mk 14:33–34).

What was the cause of this mortal dread in Jesus? We can only surmise.

1. Frightful was the anticipation of the terrible ordeal that awaited Him. Suffering, death, violent death above all, are dreaded by all men; and Jesus had the same nature as ours, but more sensitive, because more perfect, than ours.

2. More crushing, even, without any doubt, was the immense mass of sin that He took upon Himself, because He was the ransom for all sinners. "For our sakes he [God] made him to be sin who knew nothing of sin, so that in him we might become the justice of God" (2 Cor 5:21). "Christ redeemed us from the curse of the Law, becoming a curse for us; for it is written, 'Cursed is everyone who hangs on a gibbet'" (Gal 3:13).

3. The vision of souls whom He had chosen as intimate friends, especially consecrated souls, priests, religious men and

women, who prefer to feather their nests in a life of comfort, instead of helping Him save others. Did He see me among them?

4. The vision of all the souls who would be lost forever. What pain for a Christian mother to foresee the damnation of a dearly loved child! What was the agony of Jesus at the sight of those legions of condemned souls whom He loved more than the tenderest mother could, for whom He poured out His blood! A mother may always hope for a last-moment conversion. Jesus saw all those souls who were to fall certainly into the eternal flames of hell.

And among them He beheld consecrated souls, who during long years were nourished daily by His Body and Blood, who had once been generous and exemplary. They had worked zealously for the salvation of others, but in a fatal hour, because of an ill-regulated tendency, pride, or uncontrolled affection, were lost and over the centuries dragged down in their fall, directly or indirectly, hundreds, thousands, even millions of others, whom they should have led to their heavenly Father. . . .

Chapter 17

THE SORROWS OF MARY

As in the discussion of the joys of Mary, there will be question here, only of those sorrows which enable us better to understand the sorrows of Jesus.

All the sorrows of Jesus were sorrows for Mary. Would she have known them, had she not been His Mother?

Pass in review in your mind's eye the various sorrows of Jesus, and you will easily understand how each one of them induced an analogous sorrow in Mary, because, as mother, she lived only for Him and by Him, and the soul of Jesus had, so to speak, passed entirely into her. How she suffered from the ignorance and inconstancy of the crowds, from the lack of understanding of the Apostles, from the betrayal of Judas, and similar griefs.

During their hours of agony, Mother and Son were sad unto death for the same reasons, namely: the prospect of horrible torments and an agonizing death for Him whom she had brought into this world amid unspeakable joys; the thought of Jesus, purity itself, laden with the most revolting crimes of the entire human race, her sweet Jesus, "made to be sin," "becoming a curse for us"; the heart-rending spectacle of so many consecrated souls, whom Jesus had wished to make His friends and His collaborators, preferring an egoistic, sensual, easy life; the loss of those countless multitudes, casting themselves into hell, without cessation, until judgment day, and particularly the loss of consecrated souls. For all these souls she had prayed, wept, and suffered; for them she had sacrificed her Son.

It is easy to understand that if, in company with Mary, we meditate upon the sorrows of Jesus, gauging their repercussion

in the soul of Mary, they will enter our own souls more effica-
ciously. Instinctively we shall make our own the supplications
of the *Stabat Mater:*

Eia Mater, fons amoris,
Me sentire vim doloris,
Fac ut tecum lugeam.

O thou Mother, fount of love,
Touch my spirit from above,
Make my heart with thine
   accord.

Fac ut ardeat cor meum
In amando Christum Deum
Ut sibi complaceam.

Make me feel as thou hast felt;
Make my soul to glow and melt
With the love of Christ, my
   Lord.

Sancta Mater, istud agas,
Crucifixi fige plagas
Cordi meo valide.

Holy Mother, pierce me
   through,
In my heart each wound renew
Of my Savior crucified.

Tui Nati vulnerati,
Tam dignati pro me pati,
Poenas mecum divide.

Let me share with thee His
   pain,
Who for all our sins was slain,
Who for me in torments died.

Chapter 18

OUR SORROWS

Like the lives of Jesus and Mary, our lives are interwoven with joys and sorrows without number.

PERSONAL SORROWS. These can have as cause physical sufferings, such as indispositions, sickness, privations, or extremes in weather. Let us talk them over with our heavenly mother. She will invite us to contemplate Jesus in His Passion, to unite our sufferings with His, for love of Him, for love of her, for the love of souls.

There are sufferings of the heart which spring from the attitudes of those whom we love, be they members of the family, friends, or companions. They could also come from those who dislike us, or even persecute us. With Mary, let us contemplate the sufferings of Jesus due to His Mother; the sufferings of Mary due to her Son; the sorrows of Jesus due to the Apostles, the fickle, unintelligent, and ungrateful crowds, and His bitter enemies. They will teach us to accept the challenge to imitate our Master.

There are sorrows of a spiritual nature, such as temptations, dryness in prayer, feelings of utter powerlessness, of abandonment by God. With them we can go with Mary to the Garden of Olives.

Sorrows arise, too, from a lack of progress in our spiritual work or in our apostolate. United with Jesus and Mary, we can bring ourselves around to do God's will, which is the goal of all our spiritual work. With them, we succeed also in our apostolate. If our lack of success is real, it is because we have been working in our own name, not theirs. If we have worked in their name, any interruption in progress is only temporary, and guarantees future success. No one ever failed so completely as Jesus on the cross, and no one ever succeeded like Him.

SOCIAL SORROWS. There are sorrows which spring from the sorrows of others. We must know how to weep with those who mourn. (See Chapter 33, "Love for the Afflicted.")

SORROWS DUE TO JESUS AND MARY. The griefs of Jesus and Mary must be ours, too. Can we really say that we love a person if his troubles leave us indifferent as long as their cause does not bother us personally?

Jesus suffers in His Church which is His Mystical Body. The Church is the object of so much hatred in this world. The Pope, its head, is calumniated and persecuted in every age. Its bishops, its priests, religious men and women, its faithful are falsely accused, imprisoned, and even tortured.

Jesus suffers from scandals in the Church, from secret crimes, from the vulgarity, laziness, cupidity, sensuality of its consecrated souls, from the loss of so many who should have been saved, from the millions of descendants of fervent Christians who have passed over to the enemy. He suffered so much by shedding all His blood for men, and for how many He shed it in vain, just because of the disloyalty of those who had been called to be coredeemers with Himself!

The Church — that is Mary, too. The Church is our mother on earth, who continues for us the ministry of our heavenly Mother. The children of the Church are children of Mary.

Pagans, also, are her children, her children by right. For she sacrificed her Son for them also, and during the Passion she wept over them, too.

We must share the sorrows of Jesus and Mary, we must console the Redeemer and Co-redemptrix, by applying ourselves in word and act, by the reparation of suffering and by prayer, to change their sorrow into joy.

Whoever remains indifferent to the sorrows of the Church, or of Jesus and Mary, does not love them; he is just an egoist.

Chapter 19

JESUS AND THE FATHER'S WILL

THE SOUL OF JESUS IN ACCOMPLISHING HIS MISSION. The author
of the Epistle to the Hebrews indicates the glory of God as
the purpose of the Incarnation. "Therefore in coming into the
world, he [Jesus] says, 'Sacrifice and oblation thou wouldst not,
but a body thou hast fitted to me: in holocausts and sin-offerings
thou hast had no pleasure. Then said I, Behold, I come . . . to
do thy will, O God'" (Heb 10:5–7). Therefore, to offer to God
the Father a cult worthy of Him, the Second Person became
incarnate.

In St. John's Gospel, Jesus declared to Nicodemus: "For God
so loved the world that he gave his only-begotten Son, that
those who believe in him may not perish, but may have life
everlasting" (Jn 3:16). There is question here of the salvation
of men. The Nicene Creed teaches the same doctrine: *Qui
propter nos homines et propter nostram salutem descendit de
coelis* — "Who for us men, and for our salvation, came down
from heaven."

The mission of Jesus, then, deals with God and with men.
But these two ends are really one, namely, the glory of God,
brought about by the sacrifice of His Son and, thanks to this
sacrifice, the transformation of His enemies into loving children
of the Father.

We are going to contemplate the soul of Jesus in His relation to His Father and in His relation toward men.

THE SOUL OF JESUS AND THE FATHER. As we said above in
Chapter 10, from the first moment of His existence, the soul

of Jesus, in the Beatific Vision, knew God, then itself and other creatures.

It knew the three divine Persons, forming but one God.

It knew itself, a perfect creature of God, endowed with all the riches of nature and grace, substantially united, together with its body, to the Word of God, in such a way as to form a single Person with Him.

It knew all other creatures, especially rational creatures, angels and men, who were also united to the Divinity, but by a simple participation in the divine nature, and not like itself, by a substantial or hypostatic union.

The soul of Jesus, therefore, saw itself elevated to a condition infinitely higher than that of all other creatures, without merit on its part, by a pure gift of the Most Holy Trinity. And that vision filled it with an inconceivable love of God, and with an immense need to return love and gratitude by the total donation of itself to God. The soul of Jesus knew the irremediable fall of a portion of the angels. It knew the fall of the first man and of his descendants with all their crimes, and of their very material cult that was incapable of reconciling them with God. It knew, at the same time, the infinite mercy of the Creator, who was ready to pardon them and to readmit them to a union with Him by the sacrifice of His body. This knowledge gave utterance to the first word of Christ to God the Father: "A body thou hast fitted to me. . . . I come . . . to do thy will, O God" (Heb 10:5–7).

The thought of His heavenly Father, His love for the Father, His Father's glory, His desire to be consumed entirely for the Father — these were the great preoccupation, the haunting engrossment, of Jesus from the "Behold, I come" of the first moment of His life until the "It is consummated" of the very last moment. All the rest, the salvation of the world and He Himself, count only in relation to the Father.

JESUS AND THE FATHER'S WILL. "If you love me, keep my commandments," Jesus said to His disciples at the Last Supper (Jn 14:15). Love for His Father, above all, led Jesus to do everything that the Father wished. "Behold, I come, O God, to do thy will."

Another motive impelled Him, which also was a motive of love, namely, the reparation of His Father's glory, which will be treated in a later chapter.

Let us pass in review the principal occasions when Jesus had to make an act of submission to His Father's will.[1] But we must not consider only the externals in these events. We have to penetrate the soul of Jesus to discover the love, the gratitude, the self-immolation, and the joy which accompany each act of obedience. Is there joy when there are such painful emotions? Yes, joy, even in situations which entail terrible sacrifice. Sacrifice intensifies the joy, because it allows Jesus to show to advantage His love, His gratitude, and His filial submission.

If the first word which He said to His Father in this world is, "I come to do thy will," the first word which was brought to us from the Child Jesus is the declaration of His intention to be devoted entirely to His Father's business, even if He would have to cause deep anguish to the two beings who were dearest in this world, His Mother and His Foster Father (cf. Lk 2:49).

Without doubt, He was eager to start the mission which His Father had confided to Him, but He, who at twelve years had cast a spell over the doctors in the Temple of Jerusalem, waited patiently until His thirtieth year, because that was the will of His heavenly Father.

He consecrated Himself entirely to this mission, forgetting Himself to such a degree that He was not even able to take sufficient rest or to eat, for "my food is to do the will of him who sent me, to accomplish his work" (Jn 4:34). "I do always the things that are pleasing to him" (Jn 8:29).

He came to lead the whole world back to the feet of His Father. But it is clear that His Father confined Him to the narrow limits of Galilee and Judea, for He said: "I was not sent

---

[1] Some of the incidents to be cited have already been mentioned above. There, however, they were considered as demonstrating qualities of His will; here they are offered as proofs of the loving submission of Jesus to the good pleasure of His Father.

except to the lost sheep of the house of Israel" (Mt 15:24). He submits, because the Father so wills it.

We saw above with what inflexible courage, overcoming all obstacles, He accomplished that will. But it is His Passion that is the sublime drama of obedience. Hardly had He come to the Garden of Olives, when at the sight of the physical and, above all, the inner martyrdom that awaited Him, He was overwhelmed with sorrow, disgust, anguish, and fright, so that drops of blood trickled down His face and fell upon the ground. It was more than He seemed able to bear. Nature recoiled in fear. He cried out to His Father. Still, He did not say: "Father, it is too much! I did not know what awaited me when, on entering this world, I said, 'Holocausts have not been agreeable to you; O God, I come to do your will.' Just a while ago, I did not properly estimate the horror of this martyrdom, when I said to my disciples: 'I want the world to know that I love my Father. Let us leave this place!' O Father, change your decision." On the contrary, He said simply: "Father, if it is possible, let this cup pass away from me; yet not as I will, but as thou willest." After some time, he added: "My Father, if this cup cannot pass away unless I drink it, thy will be done" (Mt 26:39-42).

Then, with resolute step, He advanced to meet the band which had come out to arrest Him. Voluntarily He surrendered to His enemies. He ordered Peter, who had drawn his sword in defense: "Put back thy sword into its place. . . . How . . . are the Scriptures to be fulfilled?" (Mt 26:53.) He let Himself be bound, scourged, crowned with thorns, laden with the cross, nailed to it — all without a word of protest. It was His Father's will.

On the cross, after having given His Mother to us, in the person of His beloved disciple, He cast a last glance at the orders received from His Father, and remembered that He had to fulfill one more prophecy: "In my thirst they gave me vinegar to drink" (Ps. 68:2). John reported the scene in these words: "After this, Jesus, knowing that all things were now accomplished, that the Scripture might be fulfilled, said, 'I thirst.' Now there was standing there a vessel full of common wine; and having put a sponge soaked with the wine on a stalk of hyssop, they put it to his mouth. Therefore, when Jesus had taken the wine, he said, 'It is consummated.' And bowing his head, he gave up his spirit" (Jn 19:28–30). It was almost a cry of joy, that "It is consummated!" The Son has completely accomplished the will of His Father, so now He can surrender His spirit into His hands.

Chapter 20

MARY AND THE FATHER'S WILL

According to a number of theologians of distinction,[1] from the moment of her conception, Mary had the use of reason and free will in order to offer to God and to bring to fruition the initial plenitude of her grace. In this privilege of hers, as in all others, she resembled her Son, with these differences, that Jesus attained this knowledge in the Beatific Vision, Mary, by infused knowledge, and that from the first moment our Lord knew the Most Holy Trinity with all that was useful for Him to know about creatures, whereas Mary knew God only, probably without the distinction of Persons, and she knew herself as His creature, loved with an infinite love. That sufficed for her to respond to God's love with an exhaustive flood of love and of gratitude, with the total offering of her whole being for all that He would ever ask of her. From the Immaculate Conception on, it was her "Behold the handmaid of the Lord; be it done to me according to thy word."

As for Jesus, we must contemplate the various manifestations of Mary's submission to God's will, not so much by studying their external aspects as by trying to penetrate the soul of Mary in order to fathom the spirit of faith, gratitude, love, and happiness with which she accomplished the divine will.

Progressively, as the senses and the mind of the child become active, she understands more clearly how she is, absolutely gratuitously, the well-beloved of the heavenly Father, and how her love and gratitude toward Him, her availability to His good pleasure, grow incessantly.

She wishes to exist for God alone, and quite early under-

---

[1] Cf. Garrigou-Lagrange, *The Mother of the Savior and Our Interior Life;* E. Neubert, *Mary in Doctrine.*

stands that therefore she must remain a virgin. How could she do that, in surroundings where it is taken for granted that every girl will marry? She really does not know, but what she does know is that her resolution came from God, and that His will is enough for her.

Then the moment comes that the divine will asks that she marry Joseph. She does not understand all this, but since it is God's will, she does not have to understand. In fact, God clears up the apparent contradiction by inspiring Joseph with the desire to remain a virgin like his betrothed.

Gabriel comes to announce to her that she is to be the Mother of the Messias. She wishes everything that God wishes, but what shall she do now, since God does not contradict Himself, and He has had her vow her virginity? The angel explains that her motherhood will be the work of the Holy Spirit and therefore a motherhood both virginal and divine. What mysteries unveil themselves at this moment to her inner view: God's glory, the destiny of countless human beings, and, for her, an unspeakable dignity, but an equal responsibility and proportionate trials! The whole divine economy for heaven and earth flashes in vision before the mind's eye of this girl of fifteen, and all of it depends upon her word. Is she going to flinch or burst out into an enthusiastic transport? For those who know her, she can give only one answer, the one she always gave to God from her Immaculate Conception on: "Behold the handmaid of the Lord, be it done to me according to thy word."

At that very moment, the Word was made flesh and said to the Father: "Behold, I come, O God, to do Thy will."

The answer which she gave to Gabriel, she will give many a time again in all sorts of disconcerting circumstances.

Now she was a mother. Joseph knew nothing of what had taken place. Shouldn't she inform him? Did not her honor and that of her Son demand it? God, however, did not make a move to aid her. It was His affair. She did not want to substitute her will for His. What faith and what heroic devotion to God's holy will!

It was with the same faith and the same loving submission
to the divine will that she obeyed Caesar who obliged her to go
to Bethlehem; that she calmly saw herself refused hospitality
on the eve of her delivery, in the city of David, the ancestor
of the Messias; that she carried Him to the Temple to pay the
tribute to the priests; that she, miraculously pure as she was,
submitted to the law of purification; that, with the Infant in her
arms, she fled at night into Egypt from the usurper of the
throne of her royal ancestors!

At the age of twelve, Jesus disappeared for three days. To
the tender lament of His Mother, He answered that He had to
be about His Father's business. Mary did not understand, but
bowed in submission and kept His words in her heart, pondering over them.

She knew that He had to appear publicly in Israel to lead
His people back to their heavenly Father. Still, during long years
He remained lost in tiny Nazareth, under the guidance of
Joseph learning an ordinary trade, and then plying it as a mas-
ter craftsman. She did not say to Him as did His cousins later:
"Manifest thyself to the world" (Jn 7:5). She held her peace
and awaited God's good hour.

Finally, then, at the age of thirty, He began His mission.
After those long years of indescribable intimacy, she was going
to be alone. He left her. And she adored God's holy will.

Could she not, however, ease His task? About His birth and
His appearance among the doctors of the Temple, she knew
wonderful things, and revealing them she could have predisposed men in His favor. But since that was not God's will, she
kept it all to herself until, years after the disappearance of her
Son, a providential indication told her to make them known.

Then she understood in its accomplishment the terrifying
prophecy of old Simeon: "Behold, this child is destined for the
fall and for the rise of many in Israel, and for a sign that shall be
contradicted. And thy own soul a sword shall pierce, that the
thoughts of many hearts may be revealed" (Lk 2:34, 35). Reports, ever more alarming, came to her, above all, the rumor

that the chief priests were plotting against Him and had sworn to put Him to death. God so permitted, His ways are the best ways. She was present at the torture of her Son, she stood at the foot of the cross, and the sword pierced her heart. It had been prophesied, so it was the Father's will. And the Mother had only to repeat the same fiat: "Behold the handmaid of the Lord; be it done to me according to thy word."

Chapter 21

OUR DISPOSITIONS TOWARD THE FATHER'S WILL

We ought, like Jesus and Mary, before all else and in everything, to bring ourselves to do the Father's will. Did not the Master teach us to pray: "Our Father, who art in heaven. . . . thy will be done on earth as it is in heaven"?

To do God's will is, in practice, the highest perfection, because, what could be more perfect than, like Jesus and Mary, to do the will of the Father? The temptation to consider a multiplication of prayers and rigorous self-chastisements as perfection is a delusion of many pious persons.

To do God's will is to love Him. What Jesus said about the disciples' love for Himself applies equally to love for the Father: "If you love Him, keep His commandments" (Jn 14:15).

To do God's will is to succeed. You necessarily succeed in the supernatural field when you do God's will. The death of Jesus, accepted because the Father willed it, in the eyes of His enemies was a most pitiable failure. But no success was ever so fruitful as that failure of Jesus.

To do God's will is to prepare peace and happiness for oneself. Nothing calms the soul or renders it happy like knowing that God is pleased with it.

To do God's will is to live by faith, often heroically. What ever pleased Jesus more than encountering souls with heroic faith?

How can we know God's will? In the teachings of Holy Scripture, in the orders of authority, even if it is unbelieving, for "there exists no authority except from God" (Rom 13:1), in our duties of state, in providential indications, in the inspirations of grace. God wishes or permits everything that happens; He has His reasons for everything that He permits; and His reasons are always reasons of love. No decision, therefore, should be taken on a whim, on a mere fancy or caprice or hunch, or in self-love, camouflaged under an honorable or religious pretext. And when God's will is not clear, we must pray, reflect, and, if necessary, consult with others, to find out what He expects of us. We must not "run faster than Providence," as St. Vincent de Paul put it. Did Mary ever regret not having revealed at once to St. Joseph the mystery of her maternity?

Sometimes God's will seems to demand something that is beyond us. It is not forbidden at such times to ask Him to remove the chalice because we are too weak. It may be that He offered it only to elicit our prayers. But, like Christ, we must add, "Father, thy will be done, not mine."

At times, God asks most disconcerting things. More than once it happened to Mary. In such cases we have to give God credit for loving us, and go right ahead. Like Mary, we shall often have the experience that the most perplexing demands of God are precisely those that have produced the happiest results.

God does not command all that He wishes from us under pain of sin, but He appeals to our generosity. It is important, however, to say "Yes" to all that He asks. When the angel asked Mary to become Mother of God, she certainly did not ask whether God demanded it under pain of sin. From the moment He wished it, both for God's work and for us, she gave without hesitation. We know now what tremendous consequences flowed from that "Yes" uttered freely and unconditionally. The results are always similar, of course in a lesser degree, when men answer God's call. Every time a man acquiesces fully in God's will, without asking whether there is a strict obligation to do so, his consent is a cause of perfection for himself and of sanctification for others, often for great multitudes.

If St. Teresa of Avila had asked a priest whether it was a

sin for a nun to go to the parlor with permission and to talk about edifying matters with her visitors, he would certainly have calmed her scruples. But had she continued such visits, after Jesus had made it clear to her that she should refrain from them, would there be a *St.* Teresa, and would the Church have had those legions of Carmelites in every part of the world to give her the support of their prayers and sacrifices?

If Francis Xavier, student at the University of Paris, had been content to prepare himself for the canonry which awaited him at home, instead of listening to the continual refrain of Ignatius of Loyola, his fellow countryman, "What will it profit a man if he gains the whole world and loses his soul?" his teachers in theology at the University, without doubt, would have approved. But what would have become of those millions of pagans whom, directly or indirectly, he later conquered for Christ?

If the Little Flower of Jesus, at such an early age, became, according to St. Pius X, the greatest saint of modern times and exerted an influence on the entire world which was only short of miraculous, was it not because, among the inspirations of grace, she did not make any distinction at all between what was precept or merely counsel, and schooled herself, from the age of three, not to refuse Jesus anything? "The surest and most fruitful rule for each person is *to be faithful to his graces and to all his graces*" (Father Chaminade), and to say to God, as Mary did, "Behold the handmaid of the Lord; be it done to me according to thy word."

Chapter 22

JESUS AND THE GLORY OF THE FATHER

We have heard the author of the Epistle to the Hebrews cite, as purpose of the Incarnation, the desire of Christ to offer to His heavenly Father an oblation worthy of Him. In heaven, ever since their creation, without interruption, the faithful angels sing an eternal canticle of adoration, "Holy, holy, holy!" But on earth the great majority of men adored idols. Even those who knew the true God rendered Him only material homage, the blood of oxen, heifers, and goats. Then Christ came to offer to His Father an oblation infinitely more glorious than all the sacrifices ordered by Moses — the sacrifice of Himself.

Christ had to make that sacrifice in all justice, since God had created Him just for that. He also had to offer it out of gratitude and love, because He had been chosen for that role. He also had to offer it, of course, in reparation for the crimes of all men, His brothers.

In fact, from His birth on, the heavenly choirs sang: "Glory to God in the highest," and during His hidden life, from the Trinity on earth, which Mary and Joseph formed with Him, there arose to the heavenly Trinity such songs of praise as had never before been sung by the myriads of angelic spirits.

But it was the generality of mankind, above all the children of Israel, that Christ wished to associate with Himself in glorifying the Father. So, when the time came, He visited cities and towns, preached in synagogues and private homes, in the streets and the public squares, at the seashore, on the mountainside, and in the desert, to acquaint the Jews, His brethren, with the true manner of adoring, loving, and serving their heavenly Father. His purpose, revealed only little by little, was to inspire them with the same sentiments toward the Father as animated Himself.

His Apostles asked Him for a formula of prayer, as John had given to his followers. Prayer for the Jews — and is it not still the same for many Christians? — was to ask all sorts of favors for themselves. But Jesus taught them, first of all, to ask for the glorification of God, and to place their own personal interests only after those of the heavenly Father. When you pray, say: "Our Father who art in heaven, hallowed be thy name [let it be considered as holy]. Thy kingdom come, thy will be done on earth as it is in heaven. Give us this day our daily bread . . ." (Mt 6:9–11).

But that lesson is hardly understood by most selfish and greedy men. His zeal for the glory of the Father filled Him with indignation against those who see in religion only a convenient means to promote their earthly interests. Hence His violence toward the sellers in the Temple, who had made the Father's house, which was a house of prayer, into "a den of thieves" (Mt 21:13). Hence, too, His invectives against the Pharisees who, under the pretext of glorifying God, sought only their own glory by calling the attention of the faithful to their long prayers, their alms, and their fasting. "Well did Isaias prophesy of you hypocrites, as it is written, 'This people honors me with their lips, but their heart is far from me; but in vain do they worship me, teaching for doctrines precepts of men'" (Mk 7:6–7).

To glorify His Father, Jesus was fond of emphasizing His own dependence upon Him. True, at times He affirmed His equality with the Father, as He is the Word of God. Thus, He declared to the Jews: "I and the Father are one" (Jn 10:30). "If you knew me, you would then know my Father also" (Jn 8:19). "If you are not willing to believe me, believe the works, that you may know and believe that the Father is in me and

I in the Father" (Jn 10:38). But oftener, He admitted as man His inferiority to the Father. "The Father is greater than I" (Jn 14:28), He said to the Apostles in the Cenacle. To those who had asked the date of the end of the world, He answered: "But of that day or hour no one knows, neither the angels in heaven, nor the Son, but the Father only" (Mk 13:32). "The Son can do nothing of himself, but only what he sees the Father doing" (Jn 5:19). "The words that I speak to you I speak not on my own authority. But the Father dwelling in me, it is he who does the works" (Jn 14:10). "No one can come to me unless the Father who sent me draw him" (Jn 6:44). It is the Father also who speaks through Him: "Of myself I do nothing: but even as the Father has taught me, I speak these things" (Jn 8:28; 12:49 f.). "The word that you have heard is not mine, but the Father's who sent me" (Jn 14:24).

Jesus thanked the Father for what He had done for Him. When the disciples returned from their first mission, and recounted that even the devils were subject to them, Jesus said: "I praise thee, Father, Lord of heaven and earth, that thou didst hide these things from the wise and prudent, and didst reveal them to little ones" (Lk 10:21). And after the resurrection of Lazarus He said: "Father, I give thee thanks that thou hast heard me. Yet I knew that thou always hearest me; but because of the people who stand round, I spoke, that they may believe that thou hast sent me" (Jn 11:41).

But the glorification of the Father par excellence was, as He had already announced on entering this world, the sacrifice of Himself upon the cross. And He wished that glorification, which was of infinite value, to be continued without interruption, throughout the entire world, until the end of time. Therefore, before offering His bloody sacrifice, He decided upon its renewal by the institution of the Eucharist and of the priesthood. And so, if all angels and all men had remained faithful to their Creator, and had sung continually throughout all eternity the "Glory be to the Father, and to the Son, and to the Holy Spirit," and if there had been no sacrifice of the cross and no sacrifice of the Mass, there would have been less glory rendered to God than at present, despite all the crimes of men upon the earth and all the blasphemy of the demons and the damned in hell. Thanks to this sacrifice of Christ, the Son of God and Son of Mary!

Chapter 23

MARY AND THE GLORY OF THE FATHER

Like Jesus, from the moment that she knew herself and her Creator — doubtless, from the moment of her Immaculate Conception — Mary gave thanks to Him whose infinite goodness manifested such love to her without the least merit on her part. Now, as Pius IX in his bull, *Ineffabilis*, and Pius XII in his encyclical, *Ad coeli Reginam*, taught that "Mary, from the first moment of her conception, was filled with such an abundance of graces that she surpassed the grace of all the saints," so also the glory which she rendered to God from that moment surpassed that which all the servants of God together brought to Him.

The perfection of Mary grew with each instant, by her perfect correspondence with all the gifts of God, and so, accordingly, did the glory which she rendered to Him.

When she came to know the rest of men, and when she saw how God had been singularly much more liberal to her with His grace than to all other creatures, she found in this goodness a special, new motive for glorifying Him. Moreover, the sight of these creatures, so forgetful, so ungrateful to their heavenly Father, so selfish even in the cult that they paid to Him, urged her to make reparation for them.

The psalms held a place of importance among the prayers of the Jews. Mary loved them tenderly, as they in general expressed her intimate sentiments so well. Those which invited Israel to bless, praise, sing, and venerate God and His infinite goodness — and they are many — were especially dear to her. With what fervor she must have chanted them!

When Mary was old enough, she went to the great feasts

celebrated in the Temple of Jerusalem. She was happy there, praying to God, praising and adoring Him with the millions of pious Jews, come from every distant country to this Temple, the only one on earth where the true God was worshiped. She grieved, too, to see the priests of the true God in a cult that was only material and selfish. If she knew Malachias, the last of the prophets, with what ardent desire she must have yearned for the realization of the prophecy in which Yahwe announced: "From the rising of the sun even to the going down . . . there is offered to my name a clean oblation; for my name is great among the Gentiles" (Mal 1:11).

Then, one day, the angel Gabriel came and announced to her from Yahwe that the Messias would come, a Messias-God, and that the Most High had chosen her to be His Mother. She received the message in complete submission to the divine will, but within her heart there was an exhilaration of joy and gratitude, which she at first suppressed in order not to betray the divine mystery before time, but which she allowed to burst forth as soon as she perceived that Elizabeth was aware of the infinite grace that God had bestowed upon her. On all other occasions, when she spoke it was with extreme sobriety. But here she sang out in a complete and enthusiastic canticle, exalting the goodness of God to her, His poor handmaid, whose nothingness He had noticed, and to all those who know their own nothingness, especially to His chosen people.

From the Incarnation on, her urge to glorify God became immeasurably more intense, not only because she had been the object of such a favor from Him, but because Jesus made her share His own life and His own need to glorify the Father.

Without the least doubt, in the intimate circle of the Holy Family, Jesus spoke of the Father and showed His love for Him, and His desire to glorify Him and to see Him glorified. And then, with His Mother and St. Joseph, He recited the psalms which extol the grandeur and the goodness of the Father. His zeal for everything that interested Him who was so dear, intensified still more the fervor of those close to Him.

Like Jesus, Mary remained obscure in her little home at Nazareth. She who was to be the Queen of Angels and of Men was happy to be only a forgotten woman, about whom her fellow townsmen would say, when Jesus revealed Himself as the Messias: "Is not this the carpenter, the son of Mary?" (Mk 6:3.)

Jesus left her to begin His public mission. The first reports she had about Him were thrilling: He spoke as never man had spoken before; He worked miracles the like of which no prophet had ever performed; and the crowds followed Him with admiration. Without doubt, Mary gave thanks for all that good news, and prayerfully glorified the Father's name.

She knew, however, that her Son was to glorify the Father in an entirely different way, by the sacrifice of Himself. She was at His side at the zenith of that glorification. It was she who had furnished the Victim for the sacrifice, she who had nourished, raised, and prepared It for the day of immolation. She had to be near Jesus for the common offering, by the union of her will and her sufferings with the will and sufferings of Christ. Though she suffered without measure, she was happy at heart, for at that hour the Father received infinite glory, and she thanked Him for having been associated with the great Victim.

If we recall now that, from the first moment of her love for the Father, Mary gave more glory to God than did all the angels and saints with their songs of praise, that her glorifying the Father increased every moment, especially from the moment when Jesus communicated to her, by His physical contact, and then by His presence and His word, a participation in His own dispositions toward the Father, and that, on Calvary particularly, He associated her in the oblation for which He had come into this world — what can we say about the glory and reparation that incomparably surpassed the sum total of accumulated outrages of perfidious men and angels? What intellect, human or angelic, could ever measure that glory?

In this, as in all her other functions and prerogatives, Mary resembled her Son, with these differences that the reparation made by Jesus had infinite value, that of Mary only a value incomparably grand, and that the reparation of Jesus counted of itself, by virtue of the hypostatic union, whereas that of Mary counted only because of its union with that of her Son.

Chapter 24

THE FATHER'S GLORY AND OURSELVES

We have seen the place of the Father's glory in the preoccupations of Christ and His Mother. Jesus wishes us to reproduce all those dispositions. Mary will help us to know them better and to make them our own.

We mentioned above that, in giving to the Apostles a formula of prayer in answer to their request, Jesus gave first place to the Father's glory. When you pray, say: "Our Father who art in heaven, hallowed be thy name"; that is, may your name be treated as something holy, may it be glorified. He wishes us, therefore, to seek, first of all, the Father's glory.

The Church clearly understood this point of the Master: the great act of religion which she performs and around which all others gravitate, is the daily renewal of the sacrifice of Calvary, of the sacrifice which makes amends to the offended glory of God, and renders Him infinite honor. And the Church prescribes that, at the end of each of the one hundred and fifty psalms, which her priests recite every day, they bow reverently adding the doxology: *Gloria Patri et Filio et Spiritui Sancto, sicut erat in principio et nunc et semper, et in saecula saeculorum. Amen.*

Now we might ask whether most of the faithful have understood the intentions of Christ and of the Church, if the petitions of the second part of the Our Father, daily bread and preservation from hell and all other evil, do not appeal to them more than those of the first part. We are so selfish that our own interests are more apt to concern us than God's glory does. How many Christians think of praying to God only for their daily needs, success in their ventures, a cure, or the end of a public calamity! Even many of the so-called devout, who are really

103

interested in the future life, are, above all, solicitous about personal graces, for instance, avoidance of sin, progress in perfection, and assurance of heaven. They are quite cool toward the good or evil done in the world at large, the victories or defeats of the Church, or the souls lost or saved elsewhere. Why should they worry about the glory of God, the eternal lot of those millions of human beings for whom the Father sent His Son into the world, for whom Jesus spilled His blood, and for whom their mother suffered the cruelest martyrdom?

On the other hand, how many Catholics there still are who prefer low Masses which permit each worshiper to pray according to his own tastes, instead of the services in which the entire community takes an active part in praising God, just as if God existed only for themselves. These same persons are not far from denouncing solemn religious services, such as High Masses, processions, pilgrimages, and religious congresses, and prefer to keep to their customary practices which do not disturb their peace! Certain Catholics have to create a new spiritual attitude, in which, without forgetting their personal needs, they, like Christ and His Mother, put the interests of God before their own personal interests.

To acquire this attitude, nothing is better than the humble, loving, prayerful contemplation of the various attitudes of Jesus and Mary toward the glory of God.

This contemplation should create in us a reverent attitude of recollection and profound faith in every sacred place, particularly during the Holy Sacrifice of the Mass.

It should even move us, everywhere and in all circumstances, to glorify God by conduct worthy of a child of God, by a life of purity, of sincerity, justice, and universal charity "without fear and without reproach."

Chapter 25

THE INTIMACY OF JESUS WITH HIS FATHER

As we have said, from His conception the human intelligence of Jesus enjoyed the vision of God. From that moment on, His life was one of uninterrupted intimacy with His Father.

Jesus affirmed this constant union to the Pharisees who reproached Him with giving testimony about Himself. "And even if I do judge, my judgment is true, because I am not alone, but with me is he who sent me, the Father" (Jn 8:16). He affirmed it to the crowd in the synagogue of Capharnaum, when He promised the Holy Eucharist: "I live because of the Father" (Jn 6:57). He recalled it to the Apostles when they went down into the Garden of Olives: "Behold, the hour is coming, and has already come, for you to be scattered, each one to his own house, and to leave me alone. But I am not alone, because the Father is with me" (Jn 16:32).

Besides, He found the Father also in the world about Him. He found Him in Mary and Joseph, representatives of the Father for Him. He found Him in all men, children of His own Father, and He tried to inspire them with His confidence in the Father and His own love for Him. He found Him in all created things, in animals and plants, in the birds of the air, the sparrows on the housetop, and the lilies of the field, because the Father created them all and takes constant care of them.

If in His soul He was always in the presence of His Father, still at times He isolated Himself from men in order to give Himself completely to His company. St. Luke reports His answer to Mary after His prolonged stay in the Temple: "How is

105

it that you sought me? Did you not know that I must be about
my Father's business?" (Lk 2:49.)

At the age of thirty, before beginning His public life, Jesus
had Himself baptized in the Jordan by John. St. Luke says that
after the baptism "he was in prayer" and "heaven was opened,
and the Holy Spirit descended upon him in bodily form as a
dove, and a voice came from heaven, 'Thou art my beloved
Son, in thee I am well pleased'" (Lk 3:21 f). Then He made
a long retreat of forty days in the desert, alone with His Father
and wild beasts (cf. Lk 4:1–13; Mk 1:13).

Jesus began to work His miracles. "Great crowds gathered
together to hear him and to be cured of their sicknesses. But he
himself was in retirement in the desert, and in prayer" (Lk
5:15–16). This was a custom of Jesus. St. Luke mentions it
again, before the choice of the twelve Apostles: "He went out
to the mountain to pray, and continued all night in prayer to
God" (Lk 6:12).

Jesus prayed to the Father before working miracles, as the
Evangelists state on several occasions. Before the cure of the
deaf-mute: "Looking up to heaven, he sighed, and said to him,
'Ephpheta,' that is, 'Be thou opened'" (Mk 7:34). At the resurrection of Lazarus, He had the rock of the sepulcher removed,
lifted His eyes to heaven, and said: "Father, I give thee thanks
that thou hast heard me. Yet I knew that thou always hearest me;
but because of the people who stand round, I spoke, that they
may believe that thou hast sent me." When he had said this, he
cried with a loud voice, "Lazarus, come forth!" (Jn 11:41–43.)

He addressed a long prayer to His heavenly Father in favor
of the disciples, after the Last Supper, the "sacerdotal prayer"
(Jn 16). He prayed to the Father in His agony (Mk 14:35),
and on the cross (cf. Lk 23:34, 45).

In His prayer He relates His joys to the Father, to thank Him,
after the return of the Apostles from their first mission (cf. Mt
10:25 f), and after the resurrection of Lazarus (cf. Jn 11:41).

He tells the Father His anxieties: "Now my soul is troubled.

And what shall I say? Father, save me from this hour" (Jn 12:27). Again: "Father, if it is possible, let this cup pass away from me" (Mt 26:39).

He prayed with complete confidence. We heard Him say to His Father at the resurrection of Lazarus: "I knew that thou always hearest me." He was heard even in the Garden of Olives, since He had demanded the fulfillment of the Father's will rather than the satisfaction of His terrified human nature. He had such confidence that sometimes He simply commanded, as when He closed His "sacerdotal prayer": "Father, I will that where I am, they also whom thou hast given me may be with me; in order that they may behold my glory, which thou hast given me" (Jn 17:24).

Usually His prayer to the Father is an effusion of indescribable love. However, in the Garden "he began to feel dread and to be exceedingly troubled. And he said . . . 'My soul is sad, even unto death'" (Mk 14:33). Did that interior trial cease when, comforted by the angel, He advanced to meet His enemies? At any rate, from then on, until the end of His life, He seemed to have enjoyed a calm courage which did not leave Him for an instant. It is true that on the cross He cried out, "My God, my God, why hast thou forsaken me?" (Mt 27:46.) Missionaries in the pulpit have tried to depict the horror of that abandonment by the heavenly Father, and some of them have even supposed that Jesus suffered the pain of loss in hell. But to understand those words of Jesus, it must be remembered that they are the opening words of Psalm 21 (22) which foretells in a gripping way the various torments of Jesus on the cross: "But I am a worm, not a man. . . . All who see me scoff at me; they mock me with parted lips, they wag their heads: 'He relied on the Lord; let him deliver him, let him rescue him, if he loves him.' . . . My tongue cleaves to my jaws. . . . They have pierced my hands and my feet; I can count all my bones . . . they divide my garments among them, and for my vesture they cast lots. . . ." There is question in the psalm of an exterior abandonment into the hands of enemies, not of a real interior abandonment by God. Besides, the second part of the psalm gives God's answer to Christ's prayer: "You who fear the Lord, praise him; . . . For he has not spurned nor disdained the wretched man in his misery, nor did he turn his face away from him, but when he cried out to him he heard him. . . . All the ends of the earth shall remember and turn to the Lord; all the families of the nations shall bow down before him. . . ." It is really a psalm of confidence which ends in a shout of triumph.

Moreover, the other words of Jesus on the cross seem to indicate a peaceful abandonment to the Father's will and the same absolute confidence which He had manifested all his life. "Father, forgive them, for they do not know what they are doing" (Lk 23:34). He knows, therefore, that He has the right to ask His Father for a grace that has infinite scope. "Amen, I say to thee, this day thou shalt be with me in paradise" (Lk 23:43). That word displays the same absolute confidence in the efficacy of His prayer. "Woman, behold thy son. . . . Behold thy mother." In these simple words He makes His last testament and wills His Mother to the Church and the Church to her.

He wished to fulfill all that God, through the prophets, had foretold about Him. That was why He said, "I thirst" (Jn 18:28). He took the vinegar and in so doing accomplished the very last prophecy, conscious of having done all that the Father expected of Him, so He said, perfectly content: "It is consummated! Father, into thy hands I commend my spirit! And having said this, he expired" (Jn 19:30; Lk 23:46).

This last word of Christ corresponds to His first. On entering this world He had said, "I come to do thy will, O God." In leaving it, He practically borrowed the words of Psalm 30 (31): "Into your hands, O Lord, I commend my spirit." Instead, though, of the word, *Lord,* Jesus substituted the sweeter name, *Father,*

Chapter 26

MARY'S CHILDLIKE INTIMACY WITH
THE FATHER

From her Immaculate Conception, like Jesus, without doubt, Mary began a life of childlike intimacy with the Father. But her vision of God was not like that of Jesus. No data permit the conclusion that Mary ever enjoyed the Beatific Vision in this world; she was to be our model for a life of faith. Still, her intimacy with the Father was in all probability uninterrupted. At the highest degree of mystical life, in the "transforming union," the faithful soul feels constantly united to God as to the life of his soul. From the Immaculate Conception on, Mary's union with God had to be superior to that of the highest mystic.

Besides, Mary's intimate union with the heavenly Father was very simple. She knew Him, she loved Him, she bowed before Him, she thanked Him, she gave herself entirely to Him. Unceasingly she received new favors from Him, and corresponded accordingly.

When she came to know other men, the other children of the Father, she added to the acts just mentioned, prayers of impetration and reparation for the wayward, and, of course, special thanks for the exceptional graces which she recognized in herself.

She learned that God had promised His people a Messias, a liberator. With what burning desire she began to ask the Father to send soon Him who was to comfort the Jews and to lead back the hearts of these men to God, their Father. She begged also because she felt compelled to do so. It is an historical fact that God often disposes with special aspirations persons to

whom He has reserved a particular mission of which they have
as yet no idea.

Now suddenly Mary saw herself, through the Father's infinite
goodness, become Mother of that Messias-Liberator, Mother
of a Messias-God. That was not only a new favor beyond any
comparison, it was a new intimacy to which the Father admitted her. His little handmaiden was made God's associate
in giving birth to Christ, by a decision that He and she should
have the same Son in common. There followed, of course, a
reverent intimacy with the Son, whose Mother she had become,
and with the Holy Spirit who had raised her to that high level.
All the dispositions of Mary, such as, love, gratitude, humility,
oblation of herself, mercy toward men, received a tremendous
lift from that new role. You can read it between the lines of
her burning *Magnificat*. How often in later life she repeated
the same sentiments of that canticle to the Father, almost in
identical words.

It was not many months later that her Son, for the first time
in her presence, pronounced the name of the Father whom He
had in heaven, *Abba!* As He grew in years and wisdom and
grace, that dear name came more frequently to His lips. He
very probably did not reveal to His Mother those mysteries
whose revelation was reserved for His public life. But He surely
taught her to pray, and He prayed with her, that the name of the
Father be hallowed, that His kingdom come, that His will be
done on earth as it is in heaven. And then, together, they recited the psalms of David, their ancestor, every day, especially
on the Sabbath. In these intimate moments the sentiments of
Jesus toward His Father became Mary's sentiments; His soul,
as it were, passed entirely into the soul of His Mother.

Besides those unspeakable joys, there were for both of them
unutterable sorrows. The cause of Mary's sorrows, as of her
joys, was Jesus. If she had frequent occasion to say, "My soul
magnifies the Lord," more often she was compelled to repeat,
"Behold the handmaid of the Lord; be it done to me according

to thy word." She confided all those sorrows to the Father. Besides, even in her grief, she tasted divine consolation, that of suffering with Jesus for the Father's glory and for the redemption of men.

On Calvary, she spoke to the Father about what she saw and heard, namely, her Son stripped, nailed to the cross, hoisted above the ground, the mockery and shouts of hatred of the chief priests, the clamor of the crowd. What impressed her most, of course, were the seven last words of Jesus, their son in common.

— "Father, forgive them. . . ." She added her prayer to that of Jesus.

— "Lord, remember me. . . ." that humble, confident prayer amid the blasphemies of the mob, a consolation for both Son and Mother. She interceded for the unhappy man and was relieved by the loving response of Jesus.

— "My God, my God, why hast thou forsaken me?" She begged the Father earnestly to have pity on their Son. In those three mortal hours, she saw accomplished all the torments of the Messias that had been foretold.

— Then Jesus lowered His eyes to her and to John at her side: "Woman, behold thy son. Behold thy mother." He confided to her all mankind whom she was in the act of bringing forth to a spiritual life by her union with Him. Thirty-three years ago, the Father had confided His Son to her, His Mother. On that Good Friday, by the voice of His Son, the Father confided to her also those who had just been born her children, and she accepted them all as her children and as those of the Father, since they formed but one with their First-born.

— "I thirst." Formerly, when He was a tiny Babe, she stilled His thirst with her own milk; here at the foot of the cross, she can only beg the Father to still His burning, bodily thirst, and His far more burning thirst for souls.

— Then she heard Him utter a loud cry and say, "It is consummated; Father, into thy hands I commend my spirit." He who had been her whole reason for existence was no longer with her. But He was close to the Father who had confided Him to her.

The bodies of the crucified had to be taken down from their crosses before the Sabbath. Usually they were thrown into a common grave. Mary spoke to the Father in prayer about the body of Jesus, what was to be done with it? And suddenly, two secret disciples of Jesus, Joseph of Arimathea and Nicodemus, obtained permission from Pilate for a private burial. After three days Mary had the immense joy of seeing her Son in His glorified body.

Some forty days later, Jesus returned to His Father, leaving His Mother alone in this world. That was a sorrow to her, separation after long years of intimacy and close collaboration in the same work, which had been entrusted to them by the Father. But there was joy, too, in watching over the Church of her Son, still in its swaddling clothes, and in encouraging and instructing the Apostles.

Still she sighed for the reunion with her Son and for a meeting with that Father in whose intimacy she had lived from the very first moment of her existence, who had adopted her as His privileged daughter, who had confided to her His only Son as her Son also, and who had associated her in all the functions and privileges of this Son. . . . But finally the hour arrived when her earthly task was finished. The Father, Son, and Holy Spirit called her to Themselves. The intimacy of this world, was succeeded then by another, infinitely closer, infinitely more beatifying. . . .

Chapter 27

OUR INTIMACY WITH THE HEAVENLY FATHER

Jesus and Mary wish to pass on to us their childlike intimacy with the Father, because we, too, are His children.

Jesus wishes us to consider His Father as our Father. In the Old Testament, we find allusions to the Fatherhood of God toward men. But generally there is question of the Lord, of the Eternal, of the Almighty, of Him who commands, threatens, and punishes, of Him whose name is not to be mentioned, and the sight of whom will kill the man who sees Him passing.

But Jesus always speaks of the Father. If, rarely, He mentions the name, God, it is when referring to His nature, His attributes, or His work in general. But He uses it sparingly in explaining God's relations to us and ours with Him.

When He teaches His Apostles to pray, He has them say, not "God" or "Lord," but "Our Father who art in heaven. . . ."

The attitudes which the Apostles should take toward this Father are the very attitudes of Jesus.

Like Jesus, they should love the Father by doing His will. Like Him they must glorify the Father. We saw all this in the preceding chapters.

Like Jesus, they will have unlimited confidence in the Father. They will have such confidence in their corporal needs. "Do not be anxious for your life, what you shall eat; nor yet for your body, what you shall put on" (Mt 6:25–34). And with charming allusions to the birds of the air and the lilies of the field, He persuades them that there is nothing more natural than to abandon themselves to the all-seeing goodness of their heavenly Father. They will have confidence in that Father even in the midst of persecution. More of this later.

113

Like Jesus, they will imitate their Father. "The Son can do nothing of himself, but only what he sees the Father doing. For whatever he does, this the Son also does in like manner" (Jn 5:19). Similarly, the disciples ought to imitate the Father. "You therefore are to be perfect, even as your heavenly Father is perfect" (Mt 5:48). They should imitate the charity of the Father, and like Him, be good to all men, in order that they might be "children of the Father in heaven, who makes his sun to rise on the good and the evil, and sends rain on the just and the unjust" (Mt 5:45). "Be merciful, therefore, even as your Father is merciful" (Lk 6:36).

Like Jesus, they should speak with the Father, as children, in all simplicity. Jesus wanted public cult, an exterior ceremonial, with rites. That is why He went up to Jerusalem regularly for the great feasts. But He did not wish a merely external cult, like that of the Pharisees who, seeking not God's glory but their own, loved the prominent places in the synagogues and the corners of the market places where they could best be seen by men (cf. Mt 6:5). The disciple, on the contrary, should live in intimacy with the Father, forget himself, and give full glory to God. He suggests: "When thou prayest, go into thy room, and closing thy door, pray to thy Father in secret; and thy Father who sees in secret, will reward thee" (Mt 6:6). In the same way, they should not give alms or fast to be seen by men, but only in secret (cf. Mt 6:2–4; 16–18), because "true worshippers will worship the Father in spirit and in truth" (Jn 4:23 f). Prayer should be a real contact of the soul with God, and not mere verbosity, like the prayer of pagans, who expect results not because of the goodness of the Father, but from the number of formulas recited (cf. Mt 6:7). Christ taught His disciples that true prayer places the interests of God before personal interests, hopes for everything from God's goodness, and perseveres in asking, not because the efficacy of prayer depends upon repeated words, but because perseverance proves and intensifies confidence in the Father (cf. Lk 11:9–13).

To understand these instructions rightly and, above all, to incorporate into our attitudes toward the Father the childlike dispositions of Jesus Himself, we must contemplate them lovingly for a long time and try to enter into His soul. We must do the same with the corresponding dispositions of Mary and also enter into her soul. We must ask this grace in prayer, begging Jesus and Mary to make their own childlike dispositions pass into our hearts.

Jesus wishes to be our life. May He come then and make us live His life so completely that we can say: "It is no longer I who love the Father, it is Christ in me who loves Him."

Mary desires ardently that her children have her own dispositions toward Him whose well-beloved daughter she is. It is a great joy for her to see those children full of confidence, respect, love, and submission to such a Father. She desires it for her own sake, she desires it for the sake of Jesus, because it is her maternal mission to form us according to the model, her Firstborn Son. As filial piety toward the Father is a grace, and as all graces come to us through Mary, the Marian soul can also say — though not in the same sense as for Jesus — "It is no longer I who love the Father, it is Mary in me who loves Him." The Marian soul cannot really contemplate the filial piety of Mary toward the Father without soon feeling its attitude toward Him completely transformed.

Chapter 28

THE MISSION OF JESUS AMONG MEN,
A MISSION OF LOVE

In the beginning of this study (Chapters 11–14) we saw that
the mission of Jesus among men consists in making them sharers
of His role as Son of God. The Fathers put it this way, "God
became man that men might become God." That mission is,
above all, a mission of love, in itself, in its motives, and in its
characteristics.

A MISSION OF LOVE IN ITSELF. Every Catholic who knows his
catechism knows that the mission of Jesus among men is a mission of love, because He came among us to save us from hell
and to merit heaven for us, and to win us these benefits. He
willingly died for us. All that presupposes in Him a love for
men. True; but how many men ever stopped to ask themselves
what infinite love that supposed?

Christ is the Son of God united to a human soul and body in
such a way that the three elements form but a single person.
He determined not only to preserve men, His brothers, from the
frightful torments of an eternal hell and to win for them eternal
happiness in heaven, but He decided to do something incomparably greater for them; namely, as Son of God, become man,
He wished that we men might become Sons of God. To accomplish that, He determined to have us participate in His divine
nature. He and we are one vine, of which He is the stem and
we are the branches. The branches share the life of the stem;
members of a body share the life of the head.

As a rule, our participation in the divinity is compared to the
change effected in a bar of iron which, after some time in the
fire, itself gives out light and heat and kindles just as fire does.

Or it is compared with the quality of a crystal exposed to the sun, which shines like a sun itself. But our deification through Christ's grace is something far more intimate, for our whole inner nature is possessed and penetrated by that participation in the divinity; all the faculties of our soul, and even our body itself, are vivified by it. Christ gives to our minds certitude about divine truths of which no philosopher ever dreamed. He gives to our wills a divine power which permits us to live higher lives, lives of purity, unselfishness, devotedness, and at the same time of humility and simplicity, which are way beyond the powers of unaided human nature. To our hearts He gives a power of loving, with intensity, purity, and disinterestedness, friends, people who are indifferent, and even enemies, just as He loves us. Despite the trials and sorrows of this life, He permits them to share a peace and happiness that are not of this world, in a certain measure even His own peace and happiness. Whatever we do or suffer in union with Him is marked with merit for eternity, like whatever He did and suffered. Even to our bodies, which for many men are sources of shame and crime, He gives the gift of purity, even angelic purity, the gift of being an obedient servant of the soul.

Jesus shares with us whatever belongs to Him: His Father is our Father; His Spirit, our Spirit; His Mother, our Mother; His merits become ours; His heaven, our heaven. Moreover, He wished to give us not only all His goods, but Himself completely, His body, soul, and divinity, and to accomplish that, He instituted the Holy Eucharist.

Now to realize such a marvel, Christ wished to annihilate Himself, to assume the condition of a slave, to abase Himself still more by becoming obedient unto death, even to the death of the cross. What philosopher, poet, or novelist would ever have conceived the idea of such a gift to beings so base and so ungrateful? Was it not folly for Him to do it? Yes, the folly of love. Did He not regret it, seeing the returns from us? There was not the least regret. He repeats that folly three or four hundred thousand times each day on all the altars of the world!

MISSION OF LOVE IN HIS MOTIVES. "God is love" (1 Jn 4:8). As man, Christ reproduces His divine attributes with inconceivable perfection. His human heart, His Sacred Heart, is all love.

The Father "so loved the world that he gave his only-begotten Son, that those who believe in him may not perish, but may have life everlasting" (Jn 3:16). In loving His Father, Jesus necessarily loved those whom His Father loved so dearly.

We have admired the great preoccupation of Jesus with glorifying His Father. But the glory of the Father, as far as we are concerned, is that we, instead of being enemies, become His loving, trusting children. Christ loves us, not only on account of the Father, but with a view to the Father.

Men are His brothers. They are of His race. He is simply their oldest brother. Their misery touches Him profoundly. The horrible fate that awaits them if they do not convert appalls Him, because He knows by a divine light just what eternal damnation means. How could He not love them with a love ready to endure anything to save them from that sinister eventuality!

These men are also children of His own Mother from the moment that He became her Son. She has an immense love for them. Will He, who loves His Mother so much, not love with the same love those children who are so dear to her?

It is a law of psychology that the more a person devotes himself and suffers for another the more his love grows for him. For three years, Jesus worked, exhausted Himself, suffered, and finally died for those men, and so, even from a merely human point of view, they became ever dearer to Him.

By a sympathy, both natural and supernatural, we must try to acquire, to make our own, that love of Jesus for all men. We just do not understand anything of the words or actions of Jesus, if we have not understood the love with which His heart is filled for men, because His every word and action proceeds from that love.

Chapter 29

MARY'S MISSION, ONE OF LOVE

It is Mary's mission to give us Jesus, to make us live with His life (cf. Chapter 7). Mary is a woman, she is a mother. Instinctively, then, we understand that her mission is one of love. Every mother is love itself, the purest, the most intense and generous that there is in nature. What, then, about the most perfect mother, not in the natural, but in the supernatural, the divine order of things?

Without doubt, to the eyes of faith, the love of Jesus, even as man, surpasses without measure Mary's love. But from a sentimental point of view, Mary's love is more understandable. Jesus is a man. He not only loves, but commands, threatens, judges, and condemns. But it is faith that tells us this, not sentiment. Mary is always she who loves us. Wherever we see her, in the presence of Gabriel, of Elizabeth, of the Baptist, the shepherds, Simeon and Anna, or of the Magi, at Jerusalem, Cana, above all on Calvary, and again in the Cenacle, and now, forever in heaven, where she performs her role of Mediatrix and Distributrix of all graces — everywhere, she is Mary, our loving mother.

The motives of Mary's love for us are in part the same as those of Jesus: she loves us because the Father loves us and sent His Son to redeem us; and also the glory of the Father will be augmented if she succeeds in making us His loving children.

She loves us because her Son loves us, because He gave His life for us, because we are His brothers, because He lives in us, and because, loving us, she simply loves Him.

119

She loves us because God made her our mother, because she
suffered so much for us, and because she sacrificed her First-
born for our redemption.

Mary's love, like that of Jesus and of the Blessed Trinity, is
not only more intense, but also vastly purer than ours. We love
others for the good which we see, or think we see, in them. Jesus
and Mary love us, not only for the good they see in us, but also
and above all for the good which they desire to bestow on us,
not so much to receive as to give. A mother's love has that
characteristic disinterestedness, but even she counts upon some
return. God and Mary, on the other hand, give even when they
know there will be no return at all.

Chapter 30

OUR MISSION, ONE OF LOVE

Like Jesus and Mary, we all have a mission of love toward the rest of men. If we are other Christs, we must reproduce His dispositions; above all, that which sums up His entire life, His entire mission, namely, love. In His discourse after the Last Supper, a short while before leaving the Cenacle in order to give Himself up to death that we might live, He said solemnly to His Apostles: "My little children . . . a new commandment I give you, that you love one another; that as I have loved you, you also love one another" (Jn 13:34).

It is because He made us participants of His nature, that we live of Him, through Him, and, far more, we form with Him but one living being, only one vine of which He is the stem and we the branches, or, according to St. Paul, only one body of which we are the members. We are all one in Jesus. When we love one another, we love Jesus. And that is so true, that He declares done to Him whatever good or bad we do to our neighbor (cf. Mt 25:34-45). The great motive in our fraternal love is then, above all, our union with Jesus in His mystical body.

There are other motives for our love of one another. We have all become children of the Mother of Jesus at Nazareth and on Calvary. We are all brothers, then, not only in Jesus but in Mary. The proverb has it, "A friend of my friend is my friend." If I love the Blessed Virgin I should also love those whom she loves, her children.

Moreover, the good deeds and the merits of each of the members of the mystical body profit all the members. If I live my Christian life, if I have received special graces, I owe them,

121

after Jesus and Mary, not only to my prayers and efforts, but
also to the prayers, good works, and sufferings of the other
members of the mystical body, in virtue of what is called the
"Communion of Saints." Justice demands, then, that I also give
to those from whom I have received favors.

Why were the first Christians so remarkable for their mutual
charity? Because they recognized and loved one another in
Christ. If in our day many Christians, and even religious, understand the great law of charity so little, it is because their religion is not a Christo-centric religion.

Practically, in just what does our mission of love to our
neighbor consist? Jesus pointed it out in a formula taken from
Leviticus. To a Scribe who wished to embarrass Him by asking which was the greatest commandment, He quoted the text
on the love of God from Deuteronomy: "Hear, O Israel! The
Lord is our God, the Lord alone! Therefore, you shall love the
Lord, your God, with all your heart, and with all your soul, and
with all your strength . . ." (Dt 6:4–5), and He added something that the rabbi had not asked for: "and the second is like
it, 'You shall love your neighbor as yourself'" (Lv 19:18; Mk
12:28–31). In His Sermon on the Mount Jesus had given a
similar formula which took its inspiration also, without doubt,
from the Old Testament Book of Tobias. Tobias said to his son:
"See thou never do to another what thou wouldst hate to have
done to thee by another" (Tb 4:16). It is a just precept, but its
practice is compatible with pure egotism. Jesus made it positive
and thereby gave it an entirely different scope: "Therefore all
things whatever you would that men should do to you, even
so do you also to them; for this is the Law and the Prophets"
(Mt 7:12). But there is another formula which expresses the
characteristic law of charity of the New Testment, and which
Jesus gave as His special commandment. In His discourse after
the Last Supper, among the outpourings of His heart to the
Apostles after Judas had left the room, Jesus said: "A new com-

mandment I give you, that you love one another: that as I have loved you, you also love one another. By this will all men know that you are my disciples, if you have love for one another" (Jn 13:34–35). Shortly after, He added: "Greater love than this no one has, that one lay down his life for his friends" (Jn 15:13–14). It is therefore the love of Jesus for us that is the norm of our love for our neighbor. That is clear, because our life is the life of Jesus in us, and our neighbor is Jesus to us, Jesus with whom we constitute one single body.

The love with which we should love one another is therefore a *new* love, as Jesus pointed out expressly, and consequently, a love different from that of the pagans and even of the Jews, so different that it ought to be the characteristic mark of Christians. There is no question, then, of a love that is mere sentiment; nor of a pure philanthropy, like that of one of the characters of the Latin dramatist Terence, who said nobly but purely naturally: "I am a man and there is nothing human that is foreign to me." A disciple of Jesus would express His mind in this tenor: "I am a member of Christ and nothing that interests another member of Christ is indifferent to me," because he is aware that all men are called to become members of Christ's mystical body, since Jesus died for us all.

It was precisely in that way that the disciples of the community of Jerusalem loved one another, for they were "of one heart and one soul." So in general did the Christians of the first centuries of whom the pagans said: "See how they love one another!" We still find such a love among believers who are profoundly Christian; more frequently still, among members of a religious community who also have but one heart and one soul. But in a number of religious houses, a person might be tempted to consider the principal virtue, not fraternal charity, but the practice of austerities or the multiplication of prayers.[1] It is not penance or even the virtue of religion that is distinctive of the follower of

---

[1] This was the case among several nuns in the Carmelite convent of Lisieux at the time of St. Teresa of the Child Jesus. The saint, herself, understood the doctrine of Jesus differently from them.

Christ, but charity, mutual love after the example of the divine Master.

What the real Christian is preoccupied with is, above all, the eternal salvation of those around him. Jesus called special disciples to help in His work of saving souls. But that does not mean to say at all that those whom He did not call specially have the right to be unconcerned about the eternal lot of their brethren. Every Christian should be another Christ. And Christ said: "Love one another as I have loved you." Christ came above all not to cure the sick, raise the dead, or feed the hungry, but to redeem souls, to win eternal life for them. He said: "The second commandment is like the first: Thou shall love thy neighbor as thyself." Now the love that we should have for ourselves consists, above all, in assuring our eternal salvation. Rather than miss that life, we should be ready to sacrifice all our goods, for "What does it profit a man, if he gain the whole world, but suffer the loss of his own soul?" (Mt 16:26.) We should be ready to sacrifice an eye, a hand, a foot, or even life itself (cf. Mk 9:42-47). We should, therefore, try to assure eternal life for our neighbor, using every available opportunity. A Christian indifferent to the eternal destiny of his neighbor has the name of Christ but not the soul of Christ.

Of course this does not mean that every Christian must go out to preach. That gift is not for everybody. But everybody must be interested in the salvation of souls and must contribute to it by his conduct, his prayers, his good works, and on occasion by the right kind of advice or encouragement.

When all is said and done, there are still many Christians who do not even suspect that the most important virtue is charity, and that the very first obligation of fraternal charity is interest in the salvation of souls.

The popes of the twentieth century, especially the last two in their exhortations to Catholic Action, have frequently and insistently recalled that obligation. In his last years Pope Pius XII preached a general mobilization of Christian forces to lead back to Christ the modern world, which has been moving farther and farther away from Him. That is the "Movement for a Better World."

On February 10, 1952, he launched his first appeal by radio: "Today, give heed to a rousing call from the lips of your Father and Shepherd, from Us who cannot remain mute and inert before a world which is unconsciously walking paths which sweep on to ruin both souls and bodies, the good and the wicked, civilization and peoples. The realization of Our responsibility before God obliges Us to attempt everything, to undertake everything, in order to spare the human race so frightful a disaster.

"To share with you these anxieties of Ours, We have chosen the eve of tomorrow's feast of the Virgin of Lourdes, because it commemorates the miraculous apparitions which, almost a hundred years ago, in that century of rationalistic aberration and religious depression, were the merciful answer of God and His Heavenly Mother to the rebellion of men, an irresistible summons back to the supernatural, and the first step toward a progressive religious renascence. . . .

"Therefore, having had recourse once again to the goodness of God and the mercy of Mary, each one of the faithful and every man of good will must re-examine, with a courage worthy of the great moments of human history, what he can and must do personally, as his own contribution to the saving power of God, in order to help a world which is started, as it is today, on the road to ruin.

"The persistence of a general condition which, We do not hesitate to say, may explode at any moment, and whose origin is to be sought in the religious lukewarmness of so many, in the low moral tone of public and private life, in systematic efforts to poison simple minds, to which poison is given after their understanding of true liberty has, so to speak, been drugged — all this cannot leave good men motionless where they are, listless spectators of an onrushing future. . . .

"Now is the time to take decisive steps and to shake off this fatal lethargy! It is time for all good men, for all who are concerned with the destinies of the world, to recognize one another and tighten their ranks. . . .

"It is an entire world which must be rebuilt from its foundations, transformed from savage to human, from human to divine. . . .

"This is not the moment to discuss, to search for new principles, to fix new aims and goals. Both the one and the other, already known and substantially verified . . . await one thing only — concrete execution. . . .

"The root of modern evils and of their baneful consequences is . . . lethargy of the spirit, weakness of the will, and coldness of heart. . . .

"We sincerely hope that this mighty awakening, to which We today exhort you, fostered without delay and tenaciously executed according to the pattern marked out . . . shall be immediately imitated in other dioceses, near and far, so that our eyes shall see not only cities, but nations, continents, the entire human race return to Christ."[2]

---

[2] *Catholic Mind*, Vol. 50, June, 1952.

Chapter 31

QUALITIES OF THE LOVE OF JESUS AND MARY FOR SOULS — AND OURS

The love of Jesus for men displays a number of distinctive qualities: it is universal, generous, unselfish, patient, understanding, humble, gentle, delicate, and merciful. Mary's love for men presents the same characteristics, in the highest degree possible to a mere creature. Our love for our fellowmen should reproduce, as far as it can, the love of our divine Brother and of our mother.

Universal Love

IN JESUS. The love of Jesus embraces all men without exception. He gives Himself to all. He excludes no one, neither the inconsiderate crowds, nor indifferent listeners, nor enemies, not even the traitor. During His life He did not speak directly to pagans or to Samaritans, because He had to bring the "good news" first of all to the chosen people. Still His love went out to the gentiles, also. He manifested that already from the very beginning by the call of the Magi to His crib, and before returning to His Father, He sent His twelve Apostles to preach the Gospel and to make disciples in every country of the world (cf. Mt 28:19). Besides, the great proof of His love was not His preaching, nor His miracles, but the sacrifice of His life for all men without exception.

IN MARY. Mary's love, like that of her Son, extends to all men. It is true that Gabriel announced a Son to her, who would reign over the house of Jacob, without mentioning the rest of the world. He did so because he wished her to understand that that

Son was to be the expected Messias. But she knew from many
passages in Holy Scripture, particularly from those which she
meditated upon most frequently, the psalms and the prophet
Isaias, that all nations would benefit from the favors of the
Messias. The old priest Simeon, under the inspiration of the
Holy Spirit, announced to her that Jesus was to be "a light of
revelation to the Gentiles" (Lk 2:32), and a few days later she
saw the first fruits of these Gentiles, the Magi, present themselves to render homage to the newborn King. More and more
clearly she understood that she was to cooperate with her Son
in saving the entire world, and in bringing forth every single
human being to the true life. Even then she loved with a
maternal love those men whom she did not yet know, but of
whom she knew she was the mother. That love was to intensify
itself immeasurably upon Calvary.

OUR LOVE FOR MEN. If the soul of Jesus and of Mary passes
into us, we shall also love all men. Already in His Sermon on
the Mount, Jesus had strongly indicated the universal character
of that love which should animate His disciples: "You have
heard that it was said, 'Thou shalt love thy neighbor, and shalt
hate thy enemy.' But I say to you, love your enemies, do good
to those who hate you, and pray for those who persecute and
calumniate you, so that you may be children of your Father
in heaven, who makes his sun to rise on the good and the evil,
and sends rain on the just and the unjust. For if you love those
who love you, what reward shall you have? Do not even the
publicans do that? And if you salute your brethren only, what
are you doing more than others? Do not even the Gentiles do
that? You therefore are to be perfect, even as your heavenly
Father is perfect" (Mt 5:43-47). The profound reason for the
universality of our love, Jesus explained in the discourse after
the Last Supper: we should love all men not only because all
of them are creatures of God, but above all because Jesus died
for all of them, because God wishes the salvation of all men,
and because we should reproduce those divine dispositions. As

St. Paul said to the Galatians: "There is neither Jew nor Greek; there is neither slave nor freeman; there is neither male nor female. For you are all one in Christ Jesus" (Gal 3:28.). Christian love takes no account of the distinctions of nationality, religion, social condition, or moral worth.

To be realistic, not every man is, in fact, another Christ. But every one has a right to be. Every man has been called to become Christ, because Jesus died for that purpose. He loved us all as sinners, because He sacrificed Himself for us before we became participants of His nature, precisely *in order* to make us such participants. We too must love sinners by helping Jesus make them participants of His life.

If, therefore, a Christian excludes from his circle of love foreigners, men of different religions or of a lower social class, men who do not share his moral convictions or political views, he himself is a stranger to the love of Christ. He refuses to observe the new commandment by which Christ's followers are recognized; and even if he can maintain that he has prophesied, driven out demons, or worked miracles, at the Last Judgment Christ will say to Him: "I never knew you. Depart from me, you workers of iniquity" (Mt 7:22–23).

Generous Love

THE LOVE OF JESUS. Jesus gives and gives Himself, too, without stint. He preaches, He works miracles; above all, He gives Himself. He so spent Himself at the caprice of the inconsiderate crowds that at Nazareth they said of Him, "He has gone mad" (Mk 3:21), and His cousins tried to pull Him away. He preached all day, and at night, when others took their rest, He still instructed a timid Pharisee. He cured a very sick person who came to Him and, instead of doing it by a word or a gesture, He wished to touch him individually. He traveled continually, from north to south and south to north, across the Promised Land and even through Perea, the Decapolis, and the country of Tyre. Exhausted, He sat down on the rim of Jacob's well. "The priest is made to be devoured," saintly Father Chevrier used to say. What priest was ever devoured like Christ?

And still, all that was nothing compared with the supreme gift which He gave us, the sacrifice of His life. "Greater love than this no one has, that one lay down his life for his friends" (Jn 15:13), He had said to His Apostles in the Cenacle. Others have imitated Him in this, but what is unique about Him is that this complete sacrifice of Himself will be reproduced millions of times until the end of the world, and that in the Eucharist He is literally *devoured* by His disciples.

Generally there is joy in sacrificing oneself for others, and this joy begets further generosity. But when unspeakable grief is mingled with the sacrifice, what generosity is required to go through with it! Who will ever know the sorrows that inundated the soul of Jesus during His Passion, above all in the Garden? "He loved me and gave himself up for me" (Gal 2:20).

THE LOVE OF MARY. Mary also gave, and gave herself, without reserve. She knew that she was associated by the Father in the mission of His Son, and she is painfully happy to share His sacrifice of love. She gave more than herself, for she gave Him who is incalculably dearer to her than life. She knew from Isaias, but even more clearly from Simeon, that she was to sacrifice Him for men. Each day she repeated in a more poignant tone, "Behold the handmaid of the Lord; be it done to me according to thy word!" She climbed Calvary with her Son. There she renounced her maternal rights over Him, in order to unite her sacrifice to His and to merit life for us.

Each of the dolors of Mary is a most intense act of love, and frequent meditation on her sorrows enables us always to enter more profoundly into the abyss of her love.

OUR LOVE. The examples of Jesus and Mary show us what our love for our neighbor should be. If it is real, it will not consist only in words or gestures of politeness, in the cold alms of a piece of money, or in the occasional contribution to some charitable cause. To love is to give, particularly to give oneself, at the cost of trouble, fatigue, and time, at the sacrifice of rest, effort, courage, if need be even life, as Jesus did. John the beloved Apostle, who reported to us the teaching of the Master on love in the discourse after the Last Supper, who preached so often about love in his extreme old age, explained to us the scope of Christ's command, "Love one another as I have loved you." In the third chapter of his First Epistle, John said: "We know that we have passed from death [of sin] to life [of grace], because we love the brethren. He who does not love abides in death. . . . In this we have come to know his love, that he laid down his life for us; and we likewise ought to lay down our life for the brethren. . . . My dear children, let us not love in word, neither with the tongue, but in deed and in truth" (1 Jn 3:14–18).

Unselfish Love

THE LOVE OF JESUS. Jesus never sought Himself. St. Paul signalized that quality of Jesus, saying, "Christ did not please himself" (Rom 15:3).

He worked miracles for those who asked. He knew, however, those who would not thank Him, those who would desert Him, and those who would turn against Him. With miraculous bread He fed the crowds who, the day after, would refuse to believe His word and would leave Him indignantly (cf. Jn 6). He cleansed ten lepers, of whom only one was going to return thanks (cf. Lk 17:12–19). He treated Judas the same as the other Apostles, so that not one suspected that he was the traitor. Among the mob which shouted, "Crucify Him!" more than one, doubtless, had been the beneficiary of His goodness.

In times of stress, weariness, and misunderstanding, He did not think of going back to His Mother's Nazareth for a few days' rest, where at least she could understand Him and compensate for the bitterness He reaped elsewhere. He renounced that consolation. Carrying His cross, abandoned by friends, insulted by enemies and even by those who a few days ago had shouted, "Hosanna to the Son of David," He heard nearby a

handful of women who wept for Him. When a person suffers
unjustly, when he is abandoned by everyone, although he might
not seek comfort, he still is cheered to find an understanding
and sympathetic soul. But Jesus wanted to forgo even that
consolation. He did not count, it was for others that He lived.
Pondering over the evils that were to befall the deicidal city,
He turned toward the women and said, "Daughters of Jerusalem,
do not weep for me, but weep for yourselves and for your
children" (Lk 23:27–31). Even on the cross, in the midst of out-
rageous tortures, He forgot Himself to think only of others. His
first word was a request for pardon for His enemies. His second, the promise of paradise to the good thief. The third, a
legacy of love for His Mother and for us. Then He spoke with
His Father and said, "I thirst" to be able to fulfill the prophecy,
that is, the will of His Father, and He commended His spirit
into His hands.

MARY'S LOVE. Mary also gave, and gave herself without thought
of any return. She visited Elizabeth to offer her services to an
aged relative and to bring her joy. Later, she offered her Son
to the shepherds, to the Magi, to Simeon and Anna, to make
them happy, and not to keep her divine treasure to herself.
Years after, she forestalled embarrassment to the couple at Cana
and, without ever having seen a miracle worked by her Son,
tactfully suggested that He remedy the situation.

But more than her services, and more even than herself, she
gave her Son, her reason for being in this world, her all: first,
the day He left her to begin His public life, though she knew
He would be a sign of contradiction to great numbers; and
then, above all, in that fateful hour when He was to be im-
molated for the salvation of men, although so many would not
profit by His death.

OUR LOVE OF OTHERS. Love among men is often selfish. They
give with a sort of contract in mind, that they will be repaid:
Do ut des; that is, I am giving in order that you give in return.
The return gift need not necessarily be material. It might be
just a vain satisfaction. Jesus reproached the Pharisees for giving

alms in the synagogues and in the public squares in order to be approved by men, and He recommended that His disciples give alms so that the right hand should not know what the left was giving (cf. Mt 6:2–3).

Ordinarily, men expect at least gratitude or love in return. Gratitude is a duty, and Jesus Himself one day complained when the nine Jewish lepers who had been cured did not come back to say thanks, as their Samaritan companion had done. But that was rather to teach a lesson. Many a time He was seen heaping favors upon people who he knew would never say a word of gratitude. We do favors to others for the sake of Jesus, and it is from Him that we must expect the reward.

We might perhaps begin to do a favor out of pure love and then be tempted to continue out of selfishness. We are more easily attached to a person for whom we have done a favor than to another from whom we have received one. We can take pleasure in the love we have for him and continue loading him with favors, not for love of Jesus, but because of the pleasure we have in giving. We must be careful to love others in Jesus, with the love that Jesus has for them.

Patient Love

IN JESUS. If ever love was patient, it was that of Jesus. He was patient with the crowds who sought only material advantages, without listening at all to His message.

He was patient with the Apostles, who, despite the explanations which He gave them separately, were attached to their own worldly ideas, and practically refused to believe in His teaching on self-renunciation and suffering. They argued among themselves who was the first among them, at the very moment when He was going to deliver Himself up to death.

He was patient, in particular, with Judas whose treason He foretold one year before His death, and whom He treated with the same gentleness as He treated the others until the very last.

He was patient, above all, during the trial that led to His

martyrdom: with His accusers, His judges, His executioners. He did not utter a protest against their malice, not even an angry word, just, "Father, forgive them, for they do not know what they are doing" (Lk 23:34).

IN MARY. Her life was one of patience, like that of Jesus.

She was patient during the thirty years of hidden life, though Gabriel had foretold that her Son would sit on the throne of David, His father, and that He would reign in the house of Jacob forever. What was He waiting for, before beginning His reign?

She was patient during the three years of the public life of Jesus, with all the reports about the bad faith and the intrigues of His enemies.

She was patient, above all, during the last act of the tragedy. Poor Mother! For thirty years she had suffered martyrdom in this drama, ever since old Simeon had told her that her Son was destined for the fall and the resurrection of many in Israel, and that a sword should pierce her heart. But she knew that this was the Father's will, and, like Jesus, she wished the accomplishment of His will, no matter what it would cost.

IN US. From Jesus and Mary, we also should learn that love is patient. Patience is the mark of true love. Often it is easier to perform an act of heroic love in a critical moment than to give proof of unwearied love in a long drawn out affair. To continue doing good, to be devoted, to sacrifice oneself, without any response, without a sign of success, amid repeated disappointments — what a trial! What a temptation, at times, to quit wearing oneself out! Educators of the young, missionaries among stubborn peoples, zealous Christians trying to convert a worthy prospect know quite well what that temptation is.

The thought of Jesus and Mary will support them. It was by seeming failure all His life that Christ saved the world. Moreover, what they do for others for the sake of Jesus, they do for Jesus Himself, and if here on earth they do not see the results of their devotedness, they will contemplate it with much more joy when they come into His heavenly presence. We never fail when we work for Jesus and Mary.

Understanding Love

IN JESUS. Jesus treats each man according to his character and his personal dispositions and avoids judging or condemning indiscriminately. John, all aglow for the glory of Jesus, had just said to Him: "Master, we saw a man who was not one of our followers casting out devils in thy name, and we forbade him." But Jesus said, "Do not forbid him, because there is no one who shall work a miracle in my name, and forthwith be able to speak ill of me. For he who is not against you is for you" (Mk 9:37–39).

Nicodemus belonged to the sect of the Pharisees. But he was an honest, though timid, man. Jesus agreed to receive and instruct him at night, without reproaching him for his lack of courage. It was that coward who dared to claim from Pilate the body of Jesus. Joseph of Arimathea also belonged to a group of enemies of Jesus, as he was a member of the Great Council which condemned Jesus to death. He also was a disciple of Jesus, but secretly, for fear of the Jews. He joined Nicodemus in burying Jesus (cf. Lk 23:50–53; Jn 19:38–40).

Jesus, who condemned as an adulterer in his heart a man who looked with lust at a woman, was evidently the declared enemy of all impurity. However, seeing the real dispositions of the unfortunate woman taken in adultery and of the one who was a public sinner, He was most gentle, and refrained from condemning them (cf. Mt 5:27; Jn 8:1–11; Lk 7:36–50).

The publicans, because of their extortions, were considered public sinners. Zacchaeus was one of their chiefs at Jericho. Jesus invited Himself into his home. That caused scandal and murmuring among the crowd. Had not Christ been taken in? Still, Luke relates: "Zacchaeus stood and said to the Lord: 'Behold, Lord, I give one-half of my possessions to the poor, and if

I have defrauded anyone of anything, I restore it fourfold'"
(Lk 19:1–10).

Jewish law prescribed fasts of various kinds. The Pharisees
and the disciples of the Baptist, for different reasons, multi-
plied fast days. But Jesus did not compel his disciples to fast.
Of course, the others were scandalized. John's disciples approached Jesus and asked Him: "Why do we and the Pharisees
often fast, whereas thy disciples do not fast?" And Jesus said
to them, "Can the wedding guests mourn as long as the bridegroom is with them? But the days will come when the bridegroom shall be taken away from them, and then they will fast"
(Mt 9:14–15). Jesus is the bridegroom. His disciples are friends
of the bridegroom. When Jesus will have been put to death,
His disciples will fast. Meanwhile they are happy; there is no
fast on feast days!

The understanding of Jesus is shown particularly in how He
formed His Apostles. He instructed them gradually, revealing
only what they could grasp, postponing more difficult truths,
and promising the Holy Spirit to give them a complete understanding of whatever He had still to tell them, but which was
beyond their capacity for the moment (cf. Jn 16:12–15).

IN MARY. The delicate, loving soul of the tender Mother of
Jesus is evidently most understanding. She knows how to be
all things to all men in utter unselfishness.

The Son of God became incarnate in her. What would have
been more natural than to remain in adoration before the
Blessed Sacrament which she bore in her womb, and to isolate
herself from all but the indispensable contact with others.
Gabriel had revealed to her the miraculous maternity of her
cousin to strengthen her faith but he did not tell her to visit
her. The heart of Mary readily interpreted God's intentions and
in haste — the Gospel emphasizes the fact — she left to carry
the Messias to the happy mother and to her predestined son.

Without any doubt, Mary willingly allowed the shepherds,
the Magi, Simeon, and Anna to satisfy their desire to see the
newborn Savior and even to hold Him in their arms.

She was invited to the wedding at Cana. She, to a wedding? Oh she would decline, of course! No, she went, and even ahead of time, to lend a hand in the preparations. She foresaw early that the wine would not last. How embarrassed the young couple and their guests would be! On the other hand, such feasts could easily lead to excess in drink. The steward hints at that in his remark to the bridegroom, "Every man at first sets forth the good wine, and when they *have drunk freely* . . ." — the modern versions use this euphemism, but the Greek text of St. Luke and the Latin translation read frankly, "when they are drunk." A shortage of wine would prevent such abuses, and a little penance would not do any harm. But Mary does not reason like that. This is a wedding; a wedding day is a feast of joy, not a penitential exercise; and she turned to Jesus tactfully asking His intervention (cf. Jn 2:1–11).

It is easy to picture the Blessed Virgin in the various circumstances in which she found herself with people in need, sensing what they wanted, and contriving to aid or to comfort them. And so, ever since she left this world, whenever one of the faithful finds himself in difficulty, he turns to her instinctively. He is confident that she will understand and will come to his aid.

In Us. We, too, must have understanding for others to be able to help them or do them good. It is a very necessary quality for those who have to comfort or direct souls. Without it, a director of conscience is apt to destroy confidence or to do harm instead of good. He must consider them sympathetically, take account of their point of view, their feelings, their desires. He must be all things to all men, rejoice with those who rejoice and weep with those who mourn (cf. Rom 12:16).

No one understands a child as his mother does, as long as there is mutual confidence between them. To succeed in loving others with an understanding love, we must look at them with the eyes of their heavenly Mother, love them with her heart, wish them well with her good will, always mindful that they, too, are her tenderly loved children, to whom she wishes to do good through us.

Humble Love

IN JESUS. Jesus said to those about Him, "Learn from me, for I am meek and humble of heart" (Mt 11:29). St. Paul was deeply impressed by the humility of Christ. To urge the Philippians to humble charity toward one another, he offered the example of the divine Model: "Have this mind in you which was also in Christ Jesus, who though he was by nature God, did not consider being equal to God a thing to be clung to, but emptied himself, taking the nature of a slave and being made like unto men. And appearing in the form of a man, he humbled himself, becoming obedient unto death, even to death on a cross" (Phil 2:5-8). Without any doubt, Christ, not only as God, but even as man hypostatically united to the divinity, infinitely surpasses all men in grandeur. But as Redeemer, He made Himself the servant of all men, and therefore inferior to those He was to serve. Besides, since it was the pride of the first Adam who failed humanity, it had to be the humility of the new Adam who should redeem it. Again, the great obstacle to the reception of Christ's message was pride. Of this the Pharisees were a glaring proof. To their haughty, disdainful attitude Christ opposed simplicity and humility.

Though scion of David and of a long line of kings, Jesus chose to be born of a family of unknown persons, nobodies, and not one of them seemed to suspect His royal lineage. He learned and practiced the trade of Joseph, the carpenter. The townsmen of Nazareth saw in Him only a man of the people and turned on Him when He arrogated to Himself the role of the Messias.

During His public life, Jesus appealed to the humble, the lowly, the poor, and made Himself one with them. That was precisely one reason for His success with the crowds whom the haughtiness of the Pharisees repulsed. He did not try to mix with the influential social classes, though He did not keep His message from them.

When He preached, multitudes followed, and all were astonished at His teaching because He spoke like one having authority, and not like the Scribes (cf. Mk 1:22). On one occasion He had just driven out a demon and cured a crowd of sick, so that there was general enthusiasm about Him. Then, the next morning, instead of exploiting His triumph, He slipped away early to an isolated spot to pray. When people woke up, He was gone. Simon and His companions at last found Him and said to Him, "They are all seeking Thee." And He said to them, "Let us go into the neighboring villages and towns, that there also I may preach. For this is why I have come" (Mk 1:35–39).

Jesus drove out the unclean spirits who said they knew that He was the Son of God, and forbade them to divulge that truth. Many a time when some unfortunate begged to be cured, after granting the favor, He charged him not to say anything about it.

At Capharnaum, after the multiplication of the loaves, when the crowd was so full of enthusiasm that it wanted to make Him king, He fled into the mountains. The next day they found Him in the synagogue; but He, humanly speaking, deliberately spoiled His chances, because He turned them against Him by insisting that they would have to eat His flesh and drink His blood (cf. Jn 6).

On Palm Sunday, He accepted His glorification because the Scripture had foretold it (cf. Mt 21:4–5; Mk 11:9–12). The crowd was at the height of its enthusiasm, because many of them had seen Him raise Lazarus and others had, of course, heard of the miracle, so they wanted to acclaim Him as the Messias (cf. Jn 12:14–15). Here again He let an opportunity slip, and that triumph of some hours only rendered more humiliating the denouncement of the following Friday when, instead of Hosanna, they screamed, "Crucify Him!"

Before His accusers and judges, Jesus seemed to have lost all His resources: there were no more miracles, and there were none of those replies that had confused, humiliated, and silenced His opponents. He permitted Himself to be bound, conducted from one judge to another, scourged, crowned with thorns, ridiculed by Herod and his court, laden with His cross, stripped of His garments, nailed to the gibbet, and hoisted up to be a spectacle of derision and the butt of sarcasm and blasphemy to those whom He had so often disconcerted with overwhelming superiority. He died on that cross in utter degradation. It was His love for men that led Him to such an ignoble end, and it was by that ignominious death that He performed the greatest act of love of His entire life, the redemption of the human race.

IN MARY. Mary entered fully into the spirit of her son. Friends round about her knew nothing of her descent from King David, nor anything at all about the marvels of the Annunciation, Visitation, or of Christ's miraculous birth. She passed for an ordinary woman, and when her Son declared Himself the Messias, people asked, "Why, is not he the son of Mary?" Wherever anyone was in need she managed to bring relief, but always tactfully, as at Cana, without drawing attention to herself.

While Jesus was enjoying His greatest success, she remained alone at Nazareth. Thus, she was not present at His triumphal entry into Jerusalem. But five days later, she was next to Him on Calvary. Whoever suspected that the woman crushed with grief, at the foot of the cross on which her Son was hanging, was accomplishing at that moment the greatest act of love ever performed by a pure creature in favor of the human race? With her Son she was opening heaven to all mankind.

After that, she again disappeared. She was present in the Cenacle with her nephews and some Galilean women (cf. Acts 1:14). Later on, no doubt in answer to one of the disciples, she gave information about the human origin of Jesus, but it was not made public until she had passed from this world.

IN US. In the practice of charity, humility is of extreme importance. The proverb has it, "It's not what you give, but how you give it." That holds whether you are giving alms, advice, or a sermon. For humility is essential to kindness. From a natural point of view, whatever is given with a sense of superiority is apt to humiliate and irritate the receiver because he is made to feel a debtor. It is not astonishing, then, that such a gift does not elicit true gratitude.

From the supernatural point of view, self-satisfaction in any good done destroys or at least diminishes its value before God. We destroy by our vanity what we try to build up by our words or our devotedness. Now, pride easily insinuates itself into any act of charity. We begin with a pure intention of doing good all around us. Our success or seeming success and the praise received beget feelings of self-satisfaction in our work, and then we go on doing for ourselves what we had begun to do, originally, for God and our neighbor.

That is why it is important to contemplate, often and lovingly, the humility of Jesus and Mary in our practice of charity. We should recall, too, that what we do to our neighbor we are not doing for such and such a man, but for Jesus and we should expect our reward from Him. Accordingly, from time to time, particularly when we are dissatisfied or disappointed in our good work toward others or in our apostolate, we might ask ourselves whether we are really doing the work for Christ or for ourselves.

Gentle Love

Jesus was always gentle from the bottom of His heart. Isaias had prophesied about Him: "He was offered and he opened not his mouth; he shall be led as a sheep to the slaughter . . . and he shall not open his mouth" (Isa 53:7). His gentleness was so evident that He could proffer it as a reason for accepting His teaching, "Learn from me, for I am meek and humble of heart" (Mt 11:29).

Obviously, in the preceding pages, we brought out the gentleness of Jesus; and we shall say more in several of the following chapters.

However, on occasion, Jesus, so meek and humble of heart, permitted Himself formidable outbursts of anger. He opened His public life at Jerusalem with an angry attack against the

profaners of the Temple, and He closed His career on Palm
Sunday with a similar scene (cf. Jn 2:13-16; Mk 11:15-17). That
long series of woes against the Pharisees is unforgettable: "Woe
to you, Scribes and Pharisees, hypocrites. Woe to you . . . who
strain out the gnat but swallow the camel! . . . Woe to you . . .
who are like whited sepulchers . . . who are full of all uncleanness. . . . Woe to you . . . who are sons of those who killed the
prophets. . . . Serpents, brood of vipers, how are you to escape
the judgment of hell?" (Mt 23.)

He was angry against the cities on the lake which were unconcerned about their conversion. "Woe to thee, Corozain! woe
to thee, Bethsaida! For if in Tyre and Sidon had been worked
the miracles that have been worked in you, they would have
repented long ago in sackcloth and ashes. . . . And thou, Capharnaum, shalt thou be exalted to heaven? Thou shalt be thrust
down to hell! For if the miracles had been wrought in Sodom
that have been worked in thee, it would have remained to this
day" (Mt 11:20-24).

He even became angry at His disciples. Once it happened
when because of their lack of faith, they could not cure the
epileptic boy (cf. Mk 9:19). Another time, they drove away
the mothers who had come to have their children blessed.
Matthew and Luke say simply that Jesus nevertheless blessed
them. Mark, who had heard the incident from Peter, adds: "But
when Jesus saw them, He was indignant" (Mk 10:13-14). He
was even angry at Peter whom He had just praised for his
faith, "Get behind me, satan" (Mk 8:33).

These angry outbursts were not provoked by any personal
offense. There was no question of Himself in the two incidents
of the profaners of the Temple, but of the honor of His Father.
In the cure of the epileptic boy there was question of a want
of faith. In the reply to Peter, there was consideration of
the Father's will. In the incident about blessing the children,
spiritual values, their innocence and simplicity, were at stake.
In cursing the cities, the cause was indifference to the message
of redemption. In the invectives against the Pharisees, there was

condemnation of falsification of consciences, of wrong teaching to the crowds, and of persecution to those who came to speak in God's name.

Moreover, this anger of Jesus was completely under control. He was aroused against those who deserved censure but He always remained calm and fair. Though He was vigorous against the hypocritical Pharisees, He did not disdain to answer their questions. He even condescended privately at night to talk things over with one of them who was sincere but not too courageous. And He congratulated another who thoroughly grasped the meaning of the greatest commandment of the law, love of God and of one's neighbor. Mark related the incident graphically: "Jesus, seeing that he had answered wisely, said to him, 'Thou art not far from the kingdom of God'" (Mk 12:28-34). After having publicly scolded His disciples for their lack of faith, He gently explained privately where they failed (cf. Mt 17:20). Terrible as He showed Himself to the sellers in the Temple, immediately afterward He received kindly the blind and lame who came to Him and He cured them (cf. Mt 21:14).

In the following chapters we shall see that the Love of Jesus was delicate and merciful.

Chapter 32

LOVE FOR THE POOR

A descendant of royal lineage, Jesus chose to be poor among the poor. He was born among them under more miserable conditions than most of them. When He was offered in the Temple by His Mother, she presented to the priest the offering of the poor. He was brought up in humble surroundings, and at times had to suffer greater privations than others, for example, on His flight into Egypt. Up to the age of thirty, He worked as a poor carpenter, so that His fellow townsmen were shocked when He proclaimed Himself the Messias. During His public life He lived on alms. He died stripped of everything, on a cross, and He had to be wrapped in a borrowed burial shroud and laid in the tomb of a friend.

He felt at home among the poor and they felt at ease with Him. It was they who understood Him best, and they formed the great body of those who followed Him in all simplicity. The rich, on the contrary, the Pharisees, Sadducees, and priests, were unable to grasp His teaching, for they fought Him and ended with putting Him to death. It was to the poor that the Master made the most magnificent promises: "Blessed are you poor, for yours is the kingdom of God. Blessed are you who hunger now, for you shall be satisfied. Blessed are you who weep now, for you shall laugh" (Lk 6:21–22).

Since the end of the Captivity, there had begun among the pious Israelites a spiritual movement known as the *Anavim*, the Poor of Yahwe. They insisted on detachment from earthly

144

goods, on humility, on the interior spirit, on absolute confidence
in God, and on purity. The words of Jesus struck a sympathetic
chord among many of the listeners.

Jesus had His Apostles practice a special poverty. They had
to leave their home, their property, their employment, and live
on alms as He did. This same detachment He demanded of the
young man, who had kept all the commandments and who
wanted to be perfect. But he was rich and unable to understand
the happiness of the poor, so he went away, sad. And Jesus, who
had first looked upon him with love, said to His disciples:
"Amen I say to you, with difficulty will a rich man enter the
kingdom of heaven" (Mt 19:23).

Echoing the beatitudes proclaimed by Christ in favor of the
poor in His Sermon on the Mount were the exclamations of joy
in Mary's Magnificat, which is full of the spirit of the *Anavim*
(see above).

> "My soul magnifies the Lord,
> and my spirit rejoices in God my Savior;
> Because he has regarded the lowliness of his handmaid . . .
> he has scattered the proud in the conceit of their heart.
> He has put down the mighty from their thrones,
> and has exalted the lowly.
> He has filled the hungry with good things,
> and the rich he has sent away empty . . ." (Lk 1:46-54).

The special love of Jesus for poverty and the poor teaches us
a twofold lesson. First, we should love poverty for ourselves:
actually, if our status demands or permits it; at least in spirit,
by detachment from the goods of this world, and by renouncing
the enjoyments which money permits only to the wealthy.

Second, we should really love the poor as Jesus and Mary did,
with a love which respects them as the chosen ones of Christ,
and aids them in the conviction that whatever we do for them
we do for Jesus.

Chapter 33

LOVE FOR THE AFFLICTED

Every person in distress has a special right to the love of Jesus. His compassion excludes no one. "Come to me, all you who labor and are burdened, and I will give you rest. Take my yoke upon you, and learn from me, for I am meek and humble of heart; and you will find rest for your souls" (Mt 11:28–29). It was as though He could not bear to see a man suffer, He who was to be the "Man of Sorrows."

He was prodigal with miracles to alleviate suffering. The Evangelists describe in detail only a limited number, but He worked so many of them that often they were obliged to be content with a general mention. At sunset, the day when He preached with such authority that He impressed all His listeners in the synagogue of Capharnaum, and when He cured the mother-in-law of Peter, all three Synoptics relate that those who had been sick with various diseases brought them to Him, and He, laying His hands upon each of them, cured them (cf. Lk 4:40; Mk 1:34; Mt 8:16). On another occasion, after having chosen the Twelve, "Coming down with them, He took His stand on a level stretch, with a crowd of his disciples, and a great multitude of people from all Judea and Jerusalem, and the sea coast of Tyre and Sidon, who came to listen to him and to be healed of their diseases. And those who were troubled with unclean spirits were cured. And all the crowd were trying to touch him, for power went forth from him and healed all" (Lk 6:17–19; cf. Lk 4:18; Mt 4:23; Jn 20:30).

He worked miracles without even having been asked, because He was pained to see others suffer. St. Luke, the Evangelist of the mercy of Jesus, relates that when Jesus was going to Naim

146

with His disciples, as He drew near the gate, a dead man was being carried out, the only son of a widow. And seeing her, He had compassion on her and said, "Do not weep." Then He stopped the procession, commanded the dead man to rise, and gave him to his mother. Everybody was in admiration. But it was not admiration that Jesus sought. It was compassion that had urged Him to act.

His compassion, however, did not always elicit admiration. More often it brought on severe criticism. The same St. Luke reported two cases. "And it came to pass on another Sabbath, that he entered the synagogue and taught. And a man was there and his right hand was withered. And the Scribes and the Pharisees were watching whether he cured on the Sabbath, that they might find how to accuse him. But he knew their thoughts, and he said to the man with the withered hand, 'Arise and stand forth in the midst.' And he arose and stood forth. But Jesus said to them, 'I ask you, is it lawful on the Sabbath to do good, or to do evil? to save a life, or to destroy it?' And having looked around upon them all, he said to the man, 'Stretch forth thy hand.' And he stretched it forth, and his hand was restored. But they were filled with fury, and began to discuss among themselves what they should do to Jesus" (Lk 6:6–11). Another time "he was teaching in one of their synagogues on the Sabbath. And behold, there was a woman who for eighteen years had had a sickness caused by a spirit; and she was bent over and utterly unable to look upwards. When Jesus saw her, he called her to him and said to her, 'Woman, thou art delivered from thy infirmity.' And he laid his hands upon her, and instantly she was made straight, and glorified God. But the ruler of the synagogue, indignant that Jesus had cured on the Sabbath, addressed the crowd, saying, 'There are six days in which one ought to work; on these therefore come and be cured, and not on the Sabbath.' But the Lord answered him and said, 'Hypocrites! does not each one of you on the Sabbath loose his ox or ass from the manger, and lead it forth to water? And this woman, daughter of Abraham as she is, whom Satan has bound, lo, for eighteen years, ought not she to be loosed from this bond on the Sabbath?' And as he said these things, all his adversaries were put to shame; and the entire crowd rejoiced at the glorious things that were done by him" (Lk 13:10–17).

It was not only to raise the dead or to cure the sick that Jesus made use of His miraculous power. At the wedding of Cana, to spare the young couple embarrassment, and the guests disappointment, He changed from 130 to 175 gallons of water into excellent wine (cf. Jn 2:1–11). What touches us more, perhaps, than His promptness in comforting the unfortunate with His divine power, is His delicate use of it.

Matthew and Mark mention only the bare fact of the cure of the sick one Sabbath evening at Capharnaum. Luke adds the remark that Jesus cured them by laying hands *on each one of them* (cf. Lk 4:40). He must have been fatigued at the end of a day of preaching. He could have given them merely a general blessing and cured them all with a single word. That would have been more expeditious and imposing. But certainly the sick were happier to feel His hands cover their heads and health flow back at the moment of contact, just as pilgrims prefer an individual, personal word of encouragement and blessing from the Holy Father in Rome to a general allocution and benediction.

One day a leper presented himself to Jesus saying, "Lord, if thou wilt, thou canst make me clean." The law forbade touching a leper under penalty of incurring a legal impurity. Besides, the disgusting sight of flesh eaten away to the bone instinctively repulsed those who were well. And St. Luke specified of the sick man in question that he was "full of leprosy." But Jesus stretched out His hand and touched him, saying, " 'I will; be thou made clean.' And immediately the leprosy left him" (Lk 5:12–13).

St. Mark relates the cure of a deaf-mute who had been led to Jesus. Without doubt, He could have cured the man with a word and sent him away to continue evangelizing the crowd which surrounded Him. Instead of that, He left the crowd, and went aside with the unfortunate man, whose embryonic stuttering was

often an object of derision. He wanted to lavish on him very
particular attention. "He put his fingers into the man's ears, and
spitting, he touched his tongue. And looking up to heaven, he
sighed, and said to him, 'Ephpheta,' that is, 'Be thou opened.'
And his ears were at once opened, and the bond of his tongue
was loosed, and he began to speak correctly" (Mk 7:31–35).

Before sending the man born blind to the pool of Siloe at
Jerusalem to wash himself and thus recover his sight, Jesus
"spat on the ground and made clay with the spittle, and spread
the clay over his eyes" (Jn 9:6). After raising to life the daughter
of Jairus, Jesus saw two blind men coming toward Him, crying
out, "Have pity on us, Son of David!" And He seeing their confidence touched their eyes, saying, "Let it be done to you according to your faith." And their eyes were opened (Mt 9:27–30).
In the same way, He cured the two blind men of Jericho,
Bartimeus and his companion (Mk 10:46). "Jesus, moved with
compassion for them, touched their eyes; and at once they received their sight" (Mt 20:34). He showed even more condescension to the blind man of Bethsaida. As soon as He reached
the town with His disciples, a blind man was led to Him and
Jesus was asked to touch him. The unfortunate man had not
been born blind but had probably lost his sight accidentally.
Jesus took special interest in him. Instead of simply touching
him as He had been asked, He took the man by the hand and,
traversing the streets and lanes, led him out of the town. There
He put spittle on his eyes, imposed hands upon him, and asked
whether he saw anything. "And the man looked up, and said,
'I see men as though they were trees, but walking about.' Then
again he laid his hands upon the man's eyes, and he began to
see, and was restored so that he saw all things plainly. And he
sent him to his house, saying, 'Go to thy house, and if thou enter
the village, tell nobody' " (Mk 8:22–26).

What a joy it must have been for the unfortunate man to be
led by the hand, cured by the spittle and the twofold touch of
the hand of Him who cured all sicknesses and raised the dead!
It was the Messias, people said!

MARY AND THE UNFORTUNATE. The Gospels do not mention any particular incidents portraying the special love of Mary for the unfortunate. But they do show her giving us at the cost of tremendous sacrifices Him who came to comfort all the unfortunate of the world. They report an incident, however, which permits us to sense the feelings of her womanly and motherly heart for all human suffering, her intervention at the wedding of Cana. Jesus solved the difficulty, but the initiative belonged to Mary, evidently because God's grace urged her to become interested. That is a blueprint of what she was going to do from heaven for all unfortunates in this world until the end of time. She sees our needs, both those we open up to her and those we do not even think of showing her, she speaks of them to Jesus, for that is her heavenly mission; and Jesus accords her the favors which she solicits for us.

WE AND THE UNFORTUNATE. The example of Jesus shows us what we should do. Like Him, we must be moved by the sight of those who are suffering in body or soul, and we must contrive to bring them the necessary relief. The egoist, who is satisfied to use his wealth for his own pleasure and remains indifferent to the sufferings of others, is not a disciple of Christ, even if he has the reputation of being a practicing Catholic. Jesus mentioned that explicitly, as a warning to us. "On judgment day the King will say: 'Depart from me, accursed ones, into the everlasting fire which was prepared for the devil and his angels. For I was hungry and you did not give me to eat; I was thirsty and you gave me no drink; I was a stranger and you did not take me in; naked, and you did not clothe me; sick, and in prison, and you did not visit me.' Then they also will answer and say, 'Lord, when did we see thee hungry, or thirsty, or a stranger, or naked, or sick, or in prison, and did not minister to thee?' Then he will answer them, saying, 'Amen I say to you, as long as you did not do it for one of these least ones, you did not do it for me.' And these will go into everlasting punishment" (Mt 25:41–46).

To be Christ's disciple, it is not sufficient, from time to time to make a donation to a good cause, or to remove an eyesore, or to still the pangs of conscience by giving an alms to a woman in rags or a child covered with sores. The way Jesus treated the distressed around Him is a lesson to us. He imposed hands on each of the sick; He touched the eyes of the blind; He rubbed spittle on the ears of the deaf and the lips of the dumb; and He even caressed the rotting flesh of the leper. If we saw Jesus in the unfortunate around us, we should not hesitate to lavish similar attentions upon them.

Chapter 34

LOVE OF JESUS FOR SINNERS

More touching still is Christ's way with sinners, because they are more unfortunate than the blind and the lepers. No culprit, no matter how scandalous his life, is shut off from His love, above all, if he admits his condition. Sinners know that and are drawn to Him. The welcome which He always gave them was so unheard of among the respected religious authorities of His day that He was a scandal to them. Did He not go so far as to invite the publican Matthew into His select group of intimates, and even take a meal at his home among other guests of unsavory reputation!

While He was at table with the new Apostle, a large number of publicans and sinners sat down with Him and His disciples. Seeing this, the Pharisees said to the disciples, "Why does your master eat with publicans and sinners?" They addressed themselves to the disciples, because they had learned to their discomfort that it was dangerous to go directly to the Master. "But Jesus heard it, and said, 'It is not the healthy who need a physician, but they who are sick. But go, and learn what this means: "I desire mercy, and not sacrifice" [Os 6:6]. For I have come to call sinners, not the just'" (Mt 9:9–13).

Zacchaeus, a leading publican at Jericho, and a wealthy man, having heard that Jesus was passing through the city, climbed a sycamore to see Him go by. "And when Jesus came to the place, he looked up and saw him, and said to him, 'Zacchaeus, make haste and come down; for I must stay in thy house today.' And he made haste and came down, and welcomed him joyfully. And upon seeing it, all began to murmur, saying, 'He has gone to be the guest of a man who is a sinner.' But Zacchaeus stood and said to the Lord, 'Behold, Lord, I give one-half of my possessions to the poor, and if I have wronged anyone in anything, I restore it fourfold.' Jesus said to him, 'Today salvation has come to this house, since he, too, is a son of Abraham. For *the Son of Man came to seek and to save what was lost*'" (Lk 19:1-10).

If Jesus fulminated against sin, He was meek and even considerate with sinners, once He discovered some sense of repentance in them. He made no allusion to their life except to strengthen their good dispositions. He appraised their hidden moral resources, and knew how to make them as generous as they had been guilty. He knew just what He was doing when He invited Levi to follow Him, and when he stayed that day at Zacchaeus' house.

One day the Scribes and Pharisees brought to Him a woman caught in adultery and, in order to trap Him, asked what they should do with her, as Moses had commanded that such a one should be stoned. "But Jesus, stooping down, began to write with his finger on the ground. But when they continued asking him, he raised himself and said to them, 'Let him who is without sin among you be the first to cast a stone at her.' And again stooping down, he began to write on the ground. But hearing this, they went away, one by one, beginning with the eldest. And Jesus remained alone, with the woman standing in the midst. And Jesus, raising himself, said to her, 'Woman, where are they? Has no one condemned thee?' She said, 'No one, Lord.' Then Jesus said, 'Neither will I condemn thee. Go thy way, and from now on sin no more'" (Jn 8:1-11). Not one word of reproach, but encouragement more effective than any possible reproach!

Still more touching was the case of the pardon of the public sinner, reported by St. Luke. "Now one of the Pharisees asked him to dine with him; so he went into the house of the Pharisee and reclined at table. And behold, a woman in the town who was a sinner, upon learning that he was at table in the Pharisee's house, brought an alabaster jar of ointment; and standing behind him at his feet, she began to bathe his feet with her tears, and wiped them with the hair of her head, and kissed his feet, and anointed them with ointment. Now when the Pharisee, who had invited him, saw it, he said to himself, 'This man, were he a prophet, would surely know what kind of woman this is who is touching him, for she is a sinner.' And Jesus answered and said to him, 'Simon, I have something to say to thee.' And he said, 'Master, speak.'

"'A certain money-lender had two debtors; the one owed five hundred denarii, the other fifty. As they had no means of paying, he forgave them both. Which of them, therefore, will love him more?' Simon answered and said, 'He, I suppose, to whom he forgave more.' And he said to him, 'Thou hast judged rightly.' And turning to the woman, he said to Simon, 'Dost thou see this woman? I came into thy house; thou gavest me no water for my feet; but she has bathed my feet with tears, and has wiped them with her hair. Thou gavest me no kiss; but she, from the moment she entered, has not ceased to kiss my feet. Thou didst not anoint my head with oil; but she has anointed my feet with ointment. Wherefore I say to thee, her sins, many as they are, shall be forgiven her, because she has loved much. But he to whom little is forgiven, loves little.' And he said to her, 'Thy sins are forgiven.' And they who were at table with him began to say within themselves, 'Who is this man, who even forgives sins?' But he said to the woman, 'Thy faith has saved thee; go in peace'" (Lk 7:36–50).

St. Luke does not mention the name of the woman, a matter readily understandable. But the incident is followed immediately by the mention of the woman who followed our Lord and "who had been cured of evil spirits and infirmities," in the first place, among them, "Mary, who is called the Magdalene, from whom seven devils had gone out." The number seven denotes a fullness, a complete servitude to the evil spirits, and recalls the seven devils of which Jesus spoke in that same Gospel of St. Luke: "When an unclean spirit has gone out of a man . . . he goes and takes seven other spirits more evil than himself, and they enter

in and dwell there; and the last state of that man becomes
worse than the first" (Lk 11:24–26). The expression, "from whom
seven devils had gone out," could very well be applied to that
public sinner converted by Jesus. Besides, why had that Mary
been surnamed the Magdalene? She was, without doubt, from
Bethany, as were Lazarus and Martha, her brother and sister.
Would not that surname have been given her because she had
spent some years at Magdala, one of those resort cities on the
lake of Tiberias, with its many strangers?

An ardent, loving nature, one day she had let herself be
drawn into a life of sin. However, from home she had main-
tained a sincere faith, and she became disgusted with her sinful
way of life on hearing about the young Prophet who was so
understanding toward sinners, and flung herself at His feet in
tears. It took courage, especially to seek Him in the house of a
Pharisee, for whom a fallen woman was the most execrable of
creatures. What must she have felt on hearing Jesus take up
her defense, rank her even above His host, the sainted Pharisee,
and, far more, solemnly declare her absolved from all her life of
infamy? From that moment, she felt ready to make any sacrifice
for Him.

Jesus had understood her. He knew all the resources of love
and generosity in her unhappy soul. One day He would say to
her virgin sister, Martha, that she, Mary, had chosen the better
part which would not be taken away from her (cf. Lk 10:42).
Mary was to repeat the anointing of the feet of Jesus in the
house of Simon the Leper (cf. Jn 12:3), and Jesus was to come
to her defense when Judas and a handful of disciples, prejudiced
by his cheap remark, resented the waste occasioned by her
anointing the head and feet of Him who had so generously pardoned her. Jesus said to them, "Let her be. Why do you trouble
her? . . . Amen I say to you, wherever in the whole world this
gospel is preached, this also that she has done shall be told
in memory of her" (Mk 14:6–9). Mary was to stand at the foot
of the cross. Martha is not mentioned there. Mary was to assist at the burial, and early, when it was still dark, the morn-

ing after the Sabbath, she was to come to embalm the body
of her Master. Seeing the stone removed, she would run to
notify Peter and John, and would return to the tomb, though
she knew it was empty. Jesus appeared to her, though through
her tears she did not at once recognize Him. He said "Mary"
in the affectionate tone that she had heard many a time. Turning, she cried out "Rabboni," Master, in Hebrew (cf. Jn 20:11–16).
Next after the Blessed Virgin Mary, the loving sinner was the
first to see Jesus risen from the dead.

From His cross, Jesus saw the executioners in the process of
dividing His garments, the priests who had condemned Him
and were still mocking Him, and the crowd of the curious among
whom many had cried out "Crucify Him!" He opened His lips
not to moan or threaten, but to say, "Father, forgive them, for
they do not know what they are doing" (Lk 23:34). He knew
their guilt, but He offered His life for them, as well as for the
rest of the human race. Pleading attenuating circumstances,
He asked pardon for them.

The rulers mocked Him: "He saved others; let him save
himself, if he is the Christ, the chosen one of God" (Lk
23:35–37). The soldiers also mocked Him saying, "If Thou art
the king of the Jews, save thyself." Even the robbers, who were
crucified with Him, reproached Him in the same way (cf. Mt
27:44; Mk 15:32). However, one of them, impressed no doubt
by the calmness of Jesus and His request for pardon for His
enemies, rebuked his companion who had sneered, "If thou
art the Christ, save thyself and us!" But the other said, " 'Dost
thou not even fear God, seeing that thou art under the same
sentence? And we indeed justly, for we are receiving what our
deeds deserved; but this man has done nothing wrong.' And
he said to Jesus, 'Lord, remember me when thou comest into
thy kingdom.' And Jesus said to him, 'Amen I say to thee, this
day thou shalt be with me in paradise' " (Lk 23:39–44). Jesus
made no allusion to his past life, nor to his scoffing of a few
minutes ago, but granted immediate, complete pardon, confirmed by a solemn declaration, "Amen I say to thee. . . ."

After His resurrection, Jesus appeared to His Apostles. He did not recall, even indirectly, their grand promises of loyalty and their cowardly desertion. His only preoccupation was to convince them of the reality of His resurrection. To the one who had denied Him three times, He appeared even before showing Himself to the others (cf. Lk 24:34). In His appearance to the Eleven on the shore of the Lake of Galilee, He put a triple question to Peter: "Simon, son of John, dost thou love me more than these do?" in which the Apostle could see an allusion to his triple denial. But it was to allow him to rehabilitate himself publicly, and to be confirmed solemnly, three times, in his prerogatives as supreme pastor of Christ's flock (cf. Jn 21:11-17).

MARY'S SPECIAL LOVE FOR SINNERS. Mary could not pardon sinners by remitting their sins, as her Son did, but, like Him, she desired their conversion with all the ardor of her soul.

From before the Incarnation, at the sight of all the sins committed around her by the chosen people, Mary Immaculate must have called for, in all her desires, and by unceasing supplication, the advent of Him who was to convert Israel. When Gabriel told her that she herself was to be His Mother, and that He would be named Jesus, "Yahwe saves," she understood, even without the angel's explanation, that He would bear that name because He was to save His people from their sins (cf. Mt 1:21).

Even before the birth of Jesus, she had to help Him begin His mission when the son of Elizabeth, John the precursor, was filled with the Holy Spirit at the mere sound of her voice, and consequently was freed from original sin.

There is no doubt that during the public life of Jesus she helped in another way, by her prayers and sacrifices, to convert the multitudes, and it must have been a great consolation for her to learn of the influence that He had over sinners and the marvelous conquests that He made among them. Soon, in heaven, she was to aid Him on a still larger scale by her mission of Refuge of Sinners.

WE, SINNERS. The contemplation of the special love of Jesus
and Mary for sinners will teach us a twofold lesson, one as
sinners ourselves, and the other as Christians obliged to pre-
occupy ourselves with the salvation of sinners.

In as much as we are sinners, the attitude of Jesus and Mary
toward sinners cannot fail to inspire us with great confidence,
despite our sins; rather, because of our sins. It is not only
innocent souls who have the right to approach them with confidence. How many times Jesus repeated that He had come
precisely for sinners! Had we committed as many sins as Mary
Magdalen or the Good Thief, a real sorrow and an absolute
faith in His goodness would suffice for complete pardon. Is it
so difficult to believe that the goodness of Jesus is greater than
our wickedness? Is not access to Him much easier than it was
for Magdalen? She had to penetrate into the house of a disdainful Pharisee. All we have to do is go to Mary, who will be
happy to lead us to Jesus and to inspire us with the dispositions
of sorrow and generosity which will make Him pardon our
sins, grave and numerous though they be.

Contemplating Jesus in His relations to sinners should urge
us to a life of generosity; the more He has to pardon, the more
we ought to love. He Himself said, "He to whom little is forgiven, loves little" (Lk 7:48). For more than one great servant
of God, as for Peter and for Mary Magdalen, the very first
beginning of a life of sanctity was a sin or a series of sins confessed in all humility and confidence to Jesus. We must make
of every sin a *felix culpa*, a happy fault, because of the generous reaction that it initiates. If, after a fall, we confide in Mary,
she will make us understand how we can please Him more than
we have offended Him.

Inasmuch as we are Christians, we are obliged to be interested in the salvation of sinners (cf. Chapter 30). The attitude
of Jesus and Mary teaches us how to take hold of such work.
We must do it by kindness, understanding, patience, without
rudeness or contempt, by devotedness, self-forgetfulness, sometimes even by the sacrifice of our life, by trying to discover the

resources of faith and generosity, buried under their sins, in order to make the sinners aware of what they have and to bring out all that they are capable of; in a word, by looking at them with the eyes of Jesus and Mary and by loving them with the hearts of Jesus and Mary.

Chapter 35

LOVE OF JESUS FOR THE PURE OF HEART

Jesus, infinite purity as the Word of God, indescribable purity as man, showed a particular attraction for pure souls. He willed to be conceived and born, by a miracle of singular purity, of the Virgin of virgins. He willed to have virgins as precursor and as foster father. Among His Apostles, He loved John, the virgin Apostle, with a special love, and He confided His Virgin Mother to him. He willed that there would be, from then on, in the religion that He brought down to earth, souls who would remain virgins, souls favored by a special grace to understand what others simply could not understand (cf. Mt 19:11). Was it not also the purity of children, besides their simplicity, that made them so dear to Him?

The rich young man, who had kept all the commandments from his youth, St. Mark says, Jesus looked upon and *loved* (cf. Mk 10:21).

Still, as we have seen, Jesus did not affect the lofty scorn of the Pharisee toward those who had fallen.

MARY'S LOVE FOR PURE SOULS. Instinctively we understand that Mary, endowed from her Immaculate Conception with a purity more than angelic, preserved from all attraction to evil because free from concupiscence, that Mary, whose virginal purity had been consecrated by unequaled miracles in the conception and birth of the God of infinite purity, should share her Son's attraction for pure souls. God had also given her a virginal spouse, and Jesus had given her the virginal Apostle to be a son and guardian. She, too, must have had a special attraction toward little children.

Still, no more than her Son, did she despise those who had

made mistakes. On the contrary, without doubt, she had already received, while on earth, a special grace to inspire those souls with a disgust for their disgrace, and to attract them to a life of utter purity. We find her on Calvary at the side of the sinner of Magdala who had remained a good woman since she had repented of her sins at the feet of Jesus.

OUR LOVE FOR PURE SOULS. From Jesus and Mary we learn, first of all, to keep our own souls perfectly pure according to our state of life. Intimacy with them will enable us to share their love for the angelic virtue and their aversion for the opposite vice. It will, of itself, as we learn from the lives of certain Marian souls, diminish the violence of temptations, if not suppress them entirely. At any rate, our instinctive recourse to Jesus and Mary will give us the strength to resist all attraction for evil. We will do everything in our power to help others by our attitude, our prayers, our advice, and by showing them the marvelous strength they can have in Mary and in Jesus in the Blessed Sacrament, in order to remain pure or to rise again after falling, and to live from then on a perfectly happy life because it is perfectly pure.

Chapter 36

THE LOVE OF JESUS FOR GENEROUS SOULS

After our Lady, the most generous souls were the Apostles. The next chapter will treat of them. But besides the Apostles there were other disciples of both sexes whom Jesus loved with a particular love because they were generous.

There was Lazarus of Bethany. Jesus was fond of visiting his home, and John the Evangelist expressly wrote that Jesus loved him. Jesus even shed tears at his death, though He knew He was going to raise him from the dead, and the Jews could not help remarking, "See how he loved him" (Jn 11:5, 36). Then there were Martha and Mary, the sisters of Lazarus, and the women of Galilee who followed Him in His travels and provided for His needs.

There were also others who had not always been models, but who to repair their mistakes, loved Him so much the more generously. Such were Zacchaeus and Mary Magdalen and, without doubt, others.

MARY'S LOVE FOR GENEROUS SOULS. It was God's will that Mary remained alone at Nazareth, offering prayers and sacrifices for her Son's mission, until they met on Calvary for the supreme sacrifice. Besides St. Joseph, Mary of Cleophas, the sister-in-law of the Blessed Virgin (for Cleophas was the brother of Joseph), John the Apostle, and Mary Magdalen, we know of no other particularly generous persons among the associates of the Mother of Jesus. She must have met others at Nazareth, and later, after the death of Jesus, some who came to visit John.

Without the least doubt, she loved those whom she knew with a special love. It is psychologically impossible for a truly generous person not to feel instinctively drawn toward every other soul whom he meets in whom he recognizes the same disposition. There is such joy for a person who wishes to belong to God without reserve in meeting a friend with the same holy ambition. For Mary that joy was incomparably greater, not only because of her outstanding generosity, but more because of Jesus, to whom a generous soul brings the keenest joy, together with an extremely efficacious cooperation in His mission.

OUR GENEROSITY. We cannot contemplate the soul of Jesus for any length of time, under the guidance of Mary, without feeling urged to give ourselves unreservedly to Him who gave and sacrificed Himself for us without the least reserve. If such contemplation does not succeed in giving birth in us to such a divine ambition, then, either we did not really penetrate the soul of Jesus, or we lack all nobility of soul. Of course, we cannot expect from the very beginning to sense that generosity which follows complete unhesitant donation of oneself. But if we persevere in this contemplation, under the guidance of Mary, we shall gradually attain that complete self-oblation, which pleases Jesus and Mary so much, and enables us to gain countless souls for them.

Chapter 37

LOVE OF JESUS FOR HIS APOSTLES

Jesus loved His Apostles with a unique love. His love for them was that of a mother, tender, delicate, and anxious, and at the same time, that of a father, deep, strong, and manly. It was supernatural in its motives and purity, but very human in its manifestations. Its warmth was immediately felt by the Apostles and, like His natural and supernatural ascendancy, invincibly drew and attached them to Himself.

The multitudes heard His teaching but often did not understand it. The Apostles received private explanations.

Some of the crowd took Him for Elias, or for John the Baptist, risen from the dead, or for another prophet. To His Apostles, Jesus solemnly avowed that He was the Messias, the Son of God (cf. Mt 16:13–20).

To those outside the inner circle, Jesus was a being immeasurably beyond them, a wonder-worker, a master, a legislator, or a judge; to His Apostles, He was a friend, almost an equal. He abased Himself even to washing their feet.

To outsiders, He showed what was, so to say, external to His person, namely, His doctrine and His power; to the Apostles He revealed the most profound thoughts and emotions of His soul, His sorrows, agony, desolation, and fears (cf. Mt 26:36–45). He promised these latter a recompense incomparably superior to that reserved for the others: "Amen I say to you that you who have followed me, in the regeneration when the Son of Man shall sit on the throne of his glory, shall also sit on twelve thrones, judging the twelve tribes of Israel" (Mt 19:28).

Jesus was preoccupied with the material needs of the Apostles.

When they returned from their missions and related to Him
all that they had done and taught, He invited them to "Come
apart into a desert place and rest a while" (Mk 6:30). Again
after the Resurrection, they had spent the night on the lake
fishing, without success. They were tired and stiff. Jesus appeared to them on the shore. He questioned them and helped
them to a second miraculous catch. When they drew near Him,
they found a fire of hot coals with a fish upon them. He said
to them, "Come and breakfast." And He gave them bread and
fish (cf. Jn 21:1–15). He was on the point of making a solemn
declaration, but first He wished that their hunger be satisfied.

He was more concerned, even anxious, about their souls. With
infinite patience, He tried to form them according to His image.
They were still weak. He knew it and foresaw that they would
be scandalized by the lot which awaited them. He warned them
in advance, enumerating the trials which they would have to
endure, in order that they would not be shaken in the hour of
temptation (cf. Jn 16:1–4). He confided that He had prayed
for them, that, though they had succumbed once, victims of
self-confidence, they would end as strong men. They would be
persecuted, but there would be nothing to fear, since the Holy
Spirit would inspire them with what to say. They would be
strong with His own strength. "Take courage, I have overcome
the world" (Jn 16:33).

What anguish was His when He feared for their perseverance,
or when He was disappointed in one of them! Listen to how
He questioned the Apostles at Capharnaum, when a large number of His disciples had withdrawn and gave up following
Him: "Do you also wish to go away?" Peter assured Him of their
fidelity, but Jesus asked again: "Have I not chosen you, the
Twelve? Yet one of you is a devil" (Jn 6:66–71). And when the
traitor was about to leave to deliver Him to His enemies,
"While they were at table eating, Jesus said, 'Amen I say to
you, one of you will betray me — one who is eating with me.
. . . The Son of Man indeed goes his way, as it is written of
him; but woe to that man by whom the Son of Man is be-

trayed! It were better for that man if he had not been born'"
(Mk 14:18–21).

His love for His intimates sprang from the deepest recesses of
His soul. It shone forth in the attitude of His body, in His
movements and His looks. He merely looked upon Peter, and
that look transformed the apostate.

But Jesus nowhere displayed the depth of His love for the
Apostles more touchingly than in His discourse after the Last
Supper. He had just given them the Sacrament of His love
and made them priests and was about to give His life for
them. With an anguished heart He predicted that one of them
would betray Him. He foretold to all of them their approaching
defection. They, however, far from believing in His word and
their weakness, boasted of their bravery and loyalty. Disre-
garding their presumption, Jesus revealed that He was leaving
to prepare a place for them in His Father's home. He would return to take them to Himself. He would do everything that they
would ask in His name. He would not leave them orphans but
would send them another Comforter. Just as He was in the Father, they would be in Him and He in them. He spoke to those
cowards as though they were His equals: "No longer do I call
you servants, because the servant does not know what his
master does. But I have called you friends, because all things
that I have heard from my Father I have made known to you"
(Jn 15:15). Then He addressed His sacerdotal prayer to the
Father, in which He praised them for their fidelity — those very
ones who shortly in the Garden of Olives were to abandon
Him — and He, as it were, identified their cause with His
(cf. Jn 17).

In this tender love of Jesus for His Apostles, there was not
the least shadow of weakness. Whenever these disciples committed faults, even when their zeal for His interests was not
all for God, He did not hesitate to reprove them. He had just
declared Peter blessed for having confessed His divinity, when
He upbraided Him, "Get behind me, satan; thou art a scandal to
me." Peter had simply been interested in forestalling the evils

which the Master had said would fall upon Him in the Holy City. James and John, the two other favored Apostles, provoked by the Samaritans' refusal to show hospitality to the Master, in their zeal wanted to call down fire upon the town, "but he turned and rebuked them, saying, 'You do not know of what manner of spirit you are; for the Son of Man did not come to destroy men's lives, but to save them'" (Lk 9:51-55). Again, John the Beloved and this brother were publicly blamed by Jesus, exposed to the indignation of the other Apostles, because of their ambitious tendencies. And it is worthy of remark, that Jesus did not choose as head of His Church that Apostle who, as everybody saw and knew, was particularly dear to Him, who understood His teachings better than any other, and who alone had stood at the foot of the cross, but Peter, a man better equipped for leading and commanding.

Once a lesson was driven home and accepted, Jesus forgave and forgot. Thus it was but a short time after having publicly rebuked John for his ambition that He permitted him to rest his head on His bosom, and it was immediately after alluding to Peter's triple denial that He proclaimed him supreme shepherd of His flock.

Why that predilection of Jesus for His Apostles? The first reason has already been given, their generosity. We are perhaps more impressed by their faults, by their mundane and selfish tendencies, than by the greatness of the contribution which they made to the Master. For love of Him they left all, not only their actual possessions, but even the possibility of acquiring any in the future, devoting themselves to a life of privations and alms. And what meant more than material possessions, they left their wives and children. In what religious order, however severe it be, is one called upon to make the same sacrifice? The Church would not permit it, and our Lord had to propose it to make it legitimate. Though they took flight in the Garden of Olives, they had been sincere in protesting that they were ready to follow Jesus, even to death. They were going to protect Him against the crowd come to

arrest Him, but His attitude disconcerted them and threw
them into panic. Years later, however, they deliberately shed
their blood for Him.

There was another reason for the special love of Jesus for
His Apostles, their future cooperation in His mission. Jesus
was to shed His blood for all men and to save them all in
principle. But for the application of the grace of salvation to
each man in particular, according to God's decrees (as Pius XII
recalls in the encyclical on the Mystical Body of Christ), He
needs the cooperation of men, and in proportion to the co-
operation which they give to Him, the number of those actually
saved will be greater or smaller. He expected this co-operation
first of all from His Apostles. In them He loved not only their
personal generosity, but also the multitude of souls whom they
would help Him lead to the Father.

MARY'S SPECIAL LOVE FOR THE APOSTLES. The Gospels hardly
give us any indications at all of the possible relations between
Mary and the Apostles. Those records, however, permit us to
discover some of them. At the beginning of His public life, Jesus,
returning from the Jordan to Galilee, passed through the town
of Cana, and met His Mother. He was accompanied by the
five disciples whom He had recruited along the banks of the
river, namely, Andrew, Peter, Philip, Nathaniel, and John. Without doubt, these five, who were so enthusiastic about the young
Messias, were happy to meet the Mother of Him who had
completely conquered them, and they felt a veneration for
that Mother, so simple, so lovable, and at the same time, so
recollected and supernatural. John, particularly, must have been
impressed by her virginal look and her words. It was he who
reported the story of the miraculous change of water into wine,
and he added the remark, "This first of his signs Jesus worked
at Cana of Galilee; and he manifested his glory, and his disciples believed in him" (Jn 2:11). He had been struck by the
supernatural effect upon the Apostles, the intervention of Mary.

Then Mary disappeared until the end of the public life of
her Son. We find her again at the foot of the cross, with John,

when the Savior confided him to her as son, and her to John
as mother. Evidently John, the only Apostle present, repre-
sented them all. Mary received a special mission among them,
a motherly mission, and they were to adopt a filial attitude
toward her, continuing to be, in a way, that Son who in a few
short minutes was to die.

For the third time we find Mary among the Apostles, when,
after the Ascension of the Master, they retired to the Cenacle
to pray and to prepare for the descent of the Holy Spirit. She
was there to pray with and for them.

Probably, too, one or the other Apostle met the Mother of
Jesus later while paying a visit to St. John.

Although the Gospel is silent on this point, we are certain
that, like her son, Mary loved the Apostles with a very special
love.

First, because she shared all the dispositions of Jesus. They
who were particularly dear to the Son were equally dear to
His Mother.

Then, the same reasons made them dear to Him and to her,
namely, the outstanding generosity and the co-operation which
they lent to the mission of her Son, a mission which she shared
with Him, as Co-redemptrix at the side of the Redeemer.

Again, Mary embraced the Apostles in her universal motherhood. If she had become on Calvary — and already in a more
remote way at Nazareth — the Mother of the Apostles, she had
also become the Mother of all men, and she loved them all as
dear children, even the multitudes who were still unknown to
her. Now all these children to whom she had given life with
much anguish on Calvary were in danger of eternal damnation,
unless disciples came to bring them that saving grace which
she, together with her Son, had merited for them. With what
loving and grateful regard she must have looked upon these
men, whose words, labors, and sacrifices brought her those
multitudes to present to the Father!

THE LOVE OF JESUS AND MARY FOR THE APOSTLES OF ALL THE
AGES. Before leaving to go to the Father, Jesus made a last

recommendation to His Apostles which He concluded in these words: "Behold, I am with you all days, even unto the consummation of the world" (Mt 28:20). Then He blessed them and ascended into heaven. "With you even unto the consummation of the world"? The Eleven who were present on the mountain at that time were going to disperse in a few years, to be succeeded by other apostles until the end of time, and it is to this whole line of apostles that the recommendations, the promises, and the blessings of Christ were directed as He ascended to the Father. The direct successors of the Eleven are the bishops and priests, also all religious men and women, even contemplative religious. Because of their generosity and their labor for souls, these latter have the right to apply to themselves the loving words which Jesus addressed to His Apostles in the Cenacle after the Last Supper. For the same reasons, they can also consider themselves as privileged children of Mary.

But every true Christian ought to be an apostle, because every Christian ought to imitate Christ, the apostle *par excellence,* and because every Christian loving his neighbor as himself should, above all things, wish him, and obtain for him according to possibilities, eternal life (see above, Chapter 30).

Ever increasing numbers of Catholics, especially in Catholic Action groups, are beginning to understand their apostolic obligations. In proportion as they enter into the views of the Church of Christ, they are His elite, and may assume as said to them what was said to the Eleven.

And as Mary's reasons for loving the Apostles with a special love fuse with those of Jesus, lay apostles also have the right to believe themselves loved by the Blessed Virgin with a special love, according as they fulfill their apostolic promises. Moreover, they have the right to count on a special assistance from the Queen of Apostles.[1]

---

[1] The reader may be disappointed in not finding in this little volume some treatment of the special love of Jesus for her who is immeasurably dearer to Him than all other creatures, His Blessed Mother. The reason is that the relations between Jesus and Mary deserve separate treatment (cf. Neubert, *My Ideal, Jesus Son of Mary,* pp. 31–34).

Chapter 38

JESUS AND THE LOVE FOR ENEMIES

Jesus made enemies from the very beginning of His public ministry when, after the miracle at Cana, He went up to Jerusalem and drove the sellers from the Temple. From then on He was the "sign of contradiction" foretold by Simeon to Mary. People had to take sides, to be for or against Him. He Himself declared that "he who is not with me is against me, and he who does not gather with me scatters" (Mt 12:30). Now those who were not with Him were numerous and powerful, the Pharisees and their enemies the Sadducees, the Scribes and priests, the Herodians and members of the Sanhedrin, and the populace who shouted "Crucify Him!"

Jesus loved all these enemies, as they were the creatures of His Father, and even they had the vocation to become members of His Mystical Body.

Sometimes Jesus spoke harshly to enemies, particularly the Pharisees, but it was to put the people on guard against false doctrine and hypocritical practice. There were never words of hatred or curses, not even when, on Calvary, they mocked Him and His confidence in God the Father. His first word on the cross was in their favor, a loving word of excuse, "Father, forgive them, for they do not know what they are doing" (Lk 23:34). His second word was a word of pardon, addressed to the penitent thief, "Amen I say to thee, this day thou shalt be with me in paradise" (Lk 23:43). But better than words of pardon, Jesus offered everything for them as well as for His Apostles and His dearest friends, namely, His lifeblood in expiation for their sins. Although the Gospel says nothing about it, we can be sure that Mary made hers those dispositions of

171

Jesus in pardoning His enemies, because her mission in heaven
was to be the Mother of Mercy, and on Calvary she united her
oblation to that of her Son in expiation for the sins of the world.
Like Jesus, His disciples were to have the obligation of pardoning their enemies. It was a new precept, practically unknown, not only to pagans, but also to Jews, even the most
pious of them. How many psalms, beautiful in other respects,
breathe hatred and curses upon their enemies! But on this point
of doctrine, Christ was formal and categorical. From the beginning of His ministry, in the contrast which He made in the
Sermon on the Mount between the old law and His own, He
explained: "You have heard that it was said: 'Thou shalt love
thy neighbor, and shalt hate thy enemy.' But I say to you, love
your enemies, do good to those who hate you, and pray for
those who persecute and calumniate you, so that you may be
children of your Father in heaven, who makes his sun to rise
upon the good and the evil, and sends rain on the just and the
unjust. For if you love those who love you, what reward shall
you have? Do not even the publicans do that? And if you salute
your brethren only, what are you doing more than others? Do
not even the Gentiles do that? You therefore are to be perfect,
even as your heavenly Father is perfect" (Mt 5:43–48).

St. Luke reports the same message: "But I say to you who
are listening: Love your enemies, do good to those who hate
you. Bless those who curse you, pray for those who calumniate
you. . . . And if you love those who love you, what merit have
you? For even sinners love those who love them. And if you
do good to those who do good to you, what merit have you?
For even sinners do that. And if you lend to those from whom
you hope to receive in return, what merit have you? For even
sinners lend to sinners that they may get back as much in
return. But love your enemies; and do good, and lend, not
hoping for any return, and your reward shall be great, and you
shall be children of the Most High, for he is kind towards the
ungrateful and evil" (Lk 6:27–29, 32–35).

He comes back on that duty in the Our Father: "In this

manner therefore shall you pray: Our Father who art in heaven, hallowed be thy name. Thy kingdom come, thy will be done on earth, as it is in heaven. Give us this day our daily bread. And forgive us our debts, as we also forgive our debtors. And lead us not into temptation, but deliver us from evil." To only one of these petitions of the Our Father, Jesus adds a commentary, to that about forgiving: For if you forgive men their offenses, your heavenly Father will also forgive you your offenses. But if you do not forgive men, neither will your Father forgive you your offenses (cf. Mt 14–15). It is to be remarked that He expressed this commentary in a double form, positive and negative, which is the ordinary procedure in Hebrew to underscore an especially important idea.

Later on Peter's question on the obligation of forgiving injuries gave our Lord the opportunity of insisting strongly on the serious nature of the duty of forgiving under pain of damnation. The rabbis taught that it would be proper to pardon up to three times. Peter understood that a greater generosity was admissible in the new law, so he asked Jesus, "Lord how often shall my brother sin against me, and I forgive him? Up to seven times?" That for him was the height of nobility of soul. Jesus answered, "I do not say to thee seven times, but seventy times seven." Then He told a parable to illustrate the scope of the precept, that of the servant who owed ten thousand talents to his master. The latter, upon the servant's pleading, forgave him everything. But the pardoned man ordered a fellow servant, who owed only a hundred denarii, to be cast into prison, despite the promises of the unfortunate man eventually to pay everything. The master having heard of this cruelty, called the first servant and said: " 'Wicked servant! I forgave thee all the debt, because thou didst entreat me. Shouldst not thou also have had pity on thy fellow-servant, even as I had pity on thee?' And his master being angry, handed him over to the torturers until he should pay all that was due to him. So also my heavenly Father will do to you, if you do not forgive your brothers from your hearts" (Mt 18:21–35). These last words are to be noted,

"Forgive from your hearts." No external, formal politeness is sufficient; there must be sincere pardon to avoid hell.

The law of chastity is difficult for many people. But for a good number, the law of forgiving injuries is much more difficult. And still God wishes to forgive the offenses, infinitely graver, which we have committed against Him only on condition that we forgive the injuries received from our equals. If, to forgive our sins, Jesus had to endure His terrible Passion, has He not the right to demand that we in turn pardon others for love of Him?

Chapter 39

THE SIMPLICITY OF EVANGELICAL CHILDHOOD

The Son of God, as we have seen, came upon earth to clothe Himself in our humanity in order to make us live His divinity, so that we can say with St. Paul, "It is now no longer I that live, but Christ lives in me." But as He created us intelligent and free beings, He does not impose that deification upon us by force; He asks our co-operation with His proposal. That co-operation consists, above all, in reproducing His attitude toward His heavenly Father and toward men. That is what He most requires of us. To realize it, certain conditions must be fulfilled. From them arise other requisites to put us in the dispositions necessary to live as intensely as possible our participated life of Christ.

One day the disciples came to Jesus and asked, " 'Who then is greatest in the kingdom of heaven?' And Jesus called a little child to him, set it in the midst of them, and said, 'Amen I say to you, unless you turn and become like little children, you will not enter into the kingdom of heaven. Whoever, therefore, humbles himself as this little child, he is the greatest in the kingdom of heaven' " (Mt 18:1–4). St. Mark relates another incident which touchingly illustrates the same doctrine. Some mothers brought their little children to Him for a blessing. The disciples began to scold them. Hearing it, Jesus, ordinarily so mild, became indignant — the word is in the Gospel — and said: " 'Let the little children come to me, and do not hinder them, for of such is the kingdom of God. Amen I say to you, whoever does not accept the kingdom of God as a little child will not enter into it.' And he put his arms about them, and laying his hands upon them, he began to bless them" (Mk 10:13–16). "It is important," said Pope Benedict XV in reference to St. Teresa of the Child Jesus, "to notice the forcefulness of this divine language. It was not enough for the Son of God to affirm in a positive manner that the kingdom of heaven belongs to children or that he who becomes like a little child will be the greatest in the kingdom of heaven, but he teaches besides and in an explicit manner *exclusion* from the kingdom of all those who do not resemble little children."[1]

A child is simple. His life has not yet been complicated by sad experiences. He says what he thinks and is shocked when he hears older people tell lies.

Simplicity is the disposition of soul that goes straight to its end with the certainty of attaining it. Simplicity lies in the end and in the means. It consists in having only one end, the good, or God, and not two ends, the one professed without having it, the other had but hidden. And the simple soul goes to that end directly, not by devious ways.

Simplicity is characterized by sincerity in word. Even the enemies of Jesus recognized that sincerity in Him. The disciples of the Pharisees, having been sent with the Herodians to trip Him in His teachings, began by saying to Him: "Master, we know that thou art truthful, and that thou teachest the way of God in truth and that thou carest not for any man; for thou dost not regard the person of men. Tell us, therefore, what dost thou think. Is it lawful to give tribute to Caesar, or not?" (Mt 22:15–22.) It is that disposition, also, that Jesus demanded of His disciples. In His Sermon on the Mount, He taught them: "Let your speech be, 'Yes, yes'; 'No, no'; and whatever is beyond these comes from the evil one" (Mt 5:37). The great obstacle which Jesus encountered was not so much sin. As soon as a sin was admitted and repented, Jesus forgave it, as He did to Magdalen and the good thief. The obstacle was a certain duplicity of character, that is to say, the pursuit of a double end:

---

[1] Quoted by M. M. Philippon, O.P., in *Sainte Therese de Lisieux, Une Voie toute nouvelle*, p. 309 f.

the one proclaimed, for example, the interests of God; and the other hidden, but real, namely, seeking personal but inadmissible interests, which lead a man to falsify his conscience and to shut his eyes to the light. It was that which hardened the Master against the Pharisees. In their doctrine and in their external conduct they were nearer to Him than the publicans and sinners. But they were hypocrites, and it was their hypocrisy which Jesus attacked unceasingly.

The doctrine of Jesus cannot be accepted by such minds. Only simple souls can understand it. It was His love for simplicity that made little children so dear to Him, and which evoked that cry of joy as soon as He had seen Nathanael, "Behold a true Israelite in whom there is no guile!" (Jn 1:47.) Practically that simplicity consists in seeking only God and His good pleasure, and in trusting the heavenly Father's loving Providence for all the rest. That is the "Little Way" of St. Teresa of the Child Jesus, which led her in so short a time to such a high degree of perfection.

Society with its compromises and concessions, with its rules of etiquette and affectations, with its polished discourses and selfish pursuits, makes of simplicity a rare virtue indeed, even among persons who consider themselves upstanding Christians. To them simplicity is naïveté. St. Gregory the Great sketches a pungent parallel between the simplicity of the saints and the shrewdness of the world (Feast of St. Celestine, Pope, May 19, 5th and 6th lessons). For true Christians, it is the mark of the "children of God" (Phil 2:15). God had to raise up St. Teresa of the Child Jesus to make its importance understood again. And still, how many people are enthusiastic about the Little Flower who have not understood her message!

MARY AND SIMPLICITY. Of all mere creatures, Mary was the most simple. She was simple sometimes heroically, from her Immaculate Conception until her death. She was simple because she always sought only the good pleasure of God without any self-interest. Gabriel announced to her that she would be the mother of the Messias, the Son of God. She did not protest her unworthiness, nor her humble social standing; she did not propose others as more worthy of that function, nor was she frightened by the responsibility of such a charge; she asked but one thing — how was she expected to cooperate, since it was clear that God had suggested to her to remain a virgin. Once she had learned that the Holy Spirit would render her fruitful, she responded in all simplicity, "Behold the handmaid of the Lord; be it done to me according to thy word." Joseph was unaware of the mystery. He noticed or learned that his betrothed was pregnant. How perplexing for him! She, however, remained silent. Her person, her honor, her future were not at stake; only the will of God counted. All was in His hands. She showed the same simplicity in doing God's will when it was impossible to find lodging among the townspeople of Bethlehem; when the order was given to flee into Egypt and to return to Nazareth; when the social status of Him whom Gabriel had announced as Messias and King of Israel remained inconspicuous for years; when His public life was blocked by opposition; when He suffered His Passion and death. Always and everywhere, the Father's will had to be accomplished with the greatest simplicity and love.

OUR EVANGELICAL SIMPLICITY. Our dispositions would be the same as hers, if we sought only the will of God, manifested by the commandments of God and the Church, by our duties of state, by our legitimate religious and civil authorities, by the ordinary events of life, and if we accomplished that holy will out of love for Jesus and under the guidance of Mary. She will obtain for us the sense and the love of that simplicity which is so dear to the Savior and so suited to make us live His life.

The fruit of this simplicity and its characteristic mark will be absolute sincerity — sincerity in word and in action. There will be no hypocrisy, duplicity, dissimulation, disloyalty, cunning, and the like. There will only be the "Yes, yes; No, no" of the Savior.

Chapter 40

THE HUMILITY OF EVANGELICAL CHILDHOOD

Humility is a characteristic of evangelical childhood. A child senses his weakness. He learns it from everyday experience. He knows he can do nothing without his father or mother.

The same sense of weakness Jesus wishes to see in those who come to Him. They must have the instinctive conviction that they can do absolutely nothing, above all on the supernatural level, without Him or His Father.

Explaining to His Apostles their participation in His life by the figure of the vine and its branches, He made them understand that of themselves they were absolutely helpless. "As the branch cannot bear fruit of itself unless it remain on the vine, so neither can you unless you abide in me. I am the vine, you are the branches. He who abides in me, and I in Him, he bears much fruit; for without me you can do nothing" (Jn 15:4-5).

They heard Jesus mention several times His own dependence upon His Father. "The Father is greater than I" (Jn 14:28). "The Son can do nothing of himself, but only what he sees the Father doing" (Jn 5:19). "The Father dwelling in me, it is he who does the works" (Jn 14:10). "Of myself I do nothing; but even as the Father has taught me, I speak these things" (Jn 8:28). There are other similar statements.

The Apostles saw Him abase Himself with the humble, the disinherited, the maimed, and with all sorts of people who were despised, in order to serve them in all simplicity. They saw Him humble Himself before them to wash their feet. He demanded that same disposition in them. "Do you know what I have done to you? You call me Master and Lord, and you say

179

well, for so I am. If, therefore, I the Lord and Master have washed your feet, you also ought to wash the feet of one another. For I have given you an example, that as I have done to you, so you also should do. Amen, amen, I say to you, no servant is greater than his master, nor is one who is sent greater than he who sent him. If you know these things, blessed shall you be if you do them" (Jn 13:13–17).

He lashed out against the pride of the Pharisees at every opportunity. He exalted the humility of the publican who made the self-accusations in the Temple. He publicly shamed two of His most cherished disciples, James and John, who had desired the first place in His kingdom. We have seen how, when the disciples asked who was the greatest in the Kingdom of Heaven, he declared it was he who became a little child. When He was nailed to the cross and insulted by all His enemies, without answering a word, then, at last, they should have understood His doctrine of evangelical humility.

THE HUMILITY OF MARY. Mary always understood that doctrine. In the light of the Holy Spirit, received from her Immaculate Conception on, she sensed as perfectly natural her own nothingness: "Because he has regarded the lowliness of his handmaid . . . henceforth all generations shall call me blessed" (Lk 1:48).[1] She knew she was a servant. Mother of the Savior, she hastened to serve her old kinswoman, Elizabeth. Handmaid of the Lord and of all men, she educated her Son for the service of God and of sinners. In her mission of universal Mediatrix of Graces, is she not still a servant in heaven?

OUR HUMILITY. The teachings and the actions of Jesus and His Mother, meditated upon frequently and lovingly, will impress upon us the importance of evangelical humility. But it is not enough to recognize, before the Blessed Sacrament, that every good that we have comes to us from God, and that without Him we can do nothing. We must attain a profound conviction of these truths, so that instinctively we attribute to God all the good that there is in us, and all the good that we do to others.

---

[1] On the humility of Mary, see Neubert, *Mary in Doctrine*, pp. 222–224.

We must see at once that it is Jesus who produces fruit in us, and that He would produce much more if we were more conscious of our necessary dependence upon Him.

In our relations with God, humility means the sense of our powerlessness without Him, and of our omnipotence with Him; the sense of gratitude for graces given to us and, through us, to others; a sense of regret that, by our want of co-operation, we prevent Him from doing for us and, through us, for others, all the good that He wishes to do.

In our relations with our neighbor, humility means a sense of respect for everybody without any secret feeling of contempt. If God has given us two talents and only one of them to our neighbor, it means that freely He wished to show Himself more liberal to us. Our service will be given voluntarily, not with an air of condescension, but of simple kindness. We do to Jesus what we are doing for our neighbor, and Jesus honors us in our neighbor, by accepting the service as done to Himself.

Habitual union with Mary considerably helps the acquisition of these dispositions because, close to the Handmaid of the Lord, we find it very natural to recognize our nothingness, to feel grateful, and to serve.

Chapter 41

EVANGELICAL CONFIDENCE

A child's personal feeling of helplessness does not discourage him in the least. His mother and father are there; they love him, and to him they are all-powerful. He has limitless confidence in them.

The Christian who has understood Christ's teaching about God should have even greater confidence in his heavenly Father, for He is *infinitely* loving and powerful.

Jesus imparted this confidence in the heavenly Father to His disciples by the simplest and the most touching comparisons. "Therefore I say to you, do not be anxious for your life, what you shall eat; nor for your body, what you shall put on. The life is a greater thing than the food, and the body than the clothing. Consider the ravens: they neither sow nor reap, they have neither storeroom nor barn; yet God feeds them. Of how much more value are you than they! But which of you by being anxious about it can add to his stature a single cubit? Therefore, if you are not able to do even a very little thing, why are you anxious concerning the rest? Consider how the lilies grow; they neither toil nor spin, yet I say to you that not even Solomon in all his glory was arrayed like one of these. But if God so clothes the grass which flourishes in the field today but tomorrow is thrown into the oven, how much more you, O you of little faith! And as for you, do not seek what you shall eat, or what you shall drink; and do not exalt yourselves (for after all these things the nations of the world seek); but your Father knows that you need these things. But seek the kingdom of God, and all these things shall be given you besides" (Lk 12:22-31).

Jesus wishes that we have confidence even when miracles are necessary. To all those who came to Him to ask even extraordinary favors, He demands but one thing — faith. The father of the boy possessed by the demon begged Him, *"If thou canst do anything,* have compassion on us and help us." The man doubted and Jesus underscored his doubt. He answered, *"If thou canst believe,* all things are possible to him who believes" (Mk 9:23).

Jesus is dissatisfied when he meets with wavering faith. He severely reprimanded the disciples who had tried in vain to drive out the devil from the possessed boy: "O unbelieving generation, how long shall I be with you? How long shall I put up with you?" (Mk 9:19.) One night, under orders from Him, the disciples crossed the Lake of Tiberias. "The boat was in the midst of the sea, buffeted by the waves, for the wind was against them. But in the fourth watch of the night he came to them, walking upon the sea. And they, seeing him walking upon the sea, were greatly alarmed, and exclaimed, 'It is a ghost!' And they cried out for fear. Then Jesus immediately spoke to them, saying, 'Take courage; it is I, do not be afraid.' But Peter answered him and said, 'Lord, if it is thou, bid me come to thee over the water.' And he said, 'Come.' Then Peter got out of the boat and walked on the water to come to Jesus. But seeing the wind was strong, he was afraid; and as he began to sink he cried out, saying, 'Lord, save me!' And Jesus at once stretched forth his hand and took hold of him, saying to him, 'O thou of little faith, why didst thou doubt?'" (Mt 14:24–31.) The Master reproached him, not for having asked for so strange a miracle, which he had at once obtained by his first moment of faith, but for not having continued to believe.

On the other hand, when He encountered great faith, He was openly pleased with it. The centurion of Capharnaum had friends ask Jesus to cure his sick servant, but did not want Him to go out of His way and come to his home, since a mere word could effect the cure. Jesus was filled with admiration and said to those who were following Him, "Amen I say to you, I have

not found such great faith in Israel" (Mt 8:5–13). He showed
the same enthusiasm for the faith of the Canaanite woman,
who, without allowing herself to be rebuffed by the apparent
hardness of Jesus toward her, continued to believe in His goodness. Jesus said to her: "O woman, great is thy faith! Let it be
done to thee as thou wilt" (Mt 15:28). In the same bracket with
those statements might be placed the incident of the withered
fig tree, when Jesus remarked that with faith like a mustard
seed the Apostles could transport a mountain (cf. Mt 21:17, 19),
and the reply of Jesus to Magdalen at His feet: "Thy faith hath
saved thee; go in peace" (Lk 7:50).

THE FAITH OF MARY. The unfortunate creatures who came to
beg Jesus for favors had enough faith to obtain many cures.
Seeing the miracles without number worked by Him, they found
it easy to believe. To the incredulous Thomas Jesus said: "Because thou hast seen me, thou hast believed. Blessed are they
who have not seen, and yet have believed" (Jn 20:29). If ever
a person had to believe without seeing, it was Mary, and she
had to believe the most improbable things. She had to believe
that she a virgin would be a mother, even the Mother of God.
She had to believe that her Child, born in a stable, forced to
flee at night by a usurper of the throne of His ancestors, should
eventually sit on the throne of David. That Jesus, a child, young
man, and carpenter for thirty years in the obscure town of
Nazareth, was the Savior of His people and of the whole human
race. That He who expired between two brigands would reign
in the house of David, and that of His kingdom there would be
no end. But she believed, without the least hesitation, with an
unshakable faith, and for that reason the words of Elizabeth
to her young visitor can be applied to the latter's entire life,
"Blessed art thou who hast believed."

The theological basis of the Blessed Virgin's faith was evidently the infallibility of God who revealed those marvels to
her. But the psychological basis was her unlimited love. On the
supernatural level, to believe is to believe in love, because all
the revelations which God proposes to man's belief are revela-

tions of love. The Incarnation, Mary's vocation to the dignity of Mother of God, the Redemption, the Holy Eucharist, the sacraments, the Church — they are all manifestations of God's love. To believe them is to believe in love; to doubt them is to doubt love. Now, from her Immaculate Conception, Mary was all love, and her love always kept growing. She was able to believe in the infinite love of God who called her to be His Mother, because she always had compelled herself to love Him with all possible intensity and purity of heart. To her more than to any other person, the words of St. John are applicable: "And we have come to know, and have believed, the love that God has in our behalf" (1 Jn 4:16).

OUR LIFE OF FAITH AND CONFIDENCE. Our faith in general, like that of Mary, should be based upon the infallibility and love of God the Revealer. The more intense and the purer our love, the easier and more penetrating will be our faith.

That practical faith, which is the confidence in God upon which Jesus insisted so much in the texts cited above, psychologically also presupposes the conviction of our utter helplessness. In the Cenacle, after having said to the Apostles, "He who abides in me and I in him, he bears much fruit," Jesus immediately added, "for without me you can do nothing" (Jn 15:5). "For when I am weak, then I am strong" (2 Cor 12:10), St. Paul said. In short, it is a matter of distrusting and trusting, distrusting oneself, and trusting God.

Practically, in meditation we must penetrate deeply into the teachings of Jesus on faith and confidence, which we have just seen, like the father of the possessed boy: "I do believe; help my unbelief." We shall contemplate Mary's faith and we shall ask her to give us her unalterable faith in the heavenly Father's infinite love and omnipotence, and in that of His Son, become one of us out of sheer love. We shall habitually evaluate everything according to Christ's word, and we shall eye with suspicion the opinions of the world.

Chapter 42

TOTAL CONSECRATION AND TOTAL RENUNCIATION

Spiritual childhood, made up of simplicity, humility, and confidence, is a Christian's indispensable condition for living the life of Christ. Living Christ's life is merely being one with Him as the branch is one with the vine. That presupposes giving oneself to Christ completely, totally, without reserve, and without compromise.

The Master was very clear and most intransigent on this point: "No man can serve two masters" (Mt 6:24). "He who is not with me is against me; and he who does not gather with me scatters" (Lk 11:23).

There is no question of purely external loyalty, consisting in practices. Jesus demands constant and complete obedience to all His commands and those of the Father, which merge with His own. "Not everyone who says to me, 'Lord, Lord,' shall enter the kingdom of heaven; but he who does the will of my Father in heaven shall enter the kingdom of heaven. Many will say to me in that day, 'Lord, Lord, did we not prophesy in thy name, and cast out devils in thy name, and work many miracles in thy name?' And then I will declare to them, 'I never knew you. Depart from me, you workers of iniquity!' " (Mt 7:21-23.) "He who has my commandments and keeps them, he it is who loves me" (Jn 14:21).

Jesus demanded blind obedience, not only to His commandments, but also to His doctrine, no matter how strange, how amazing it might appear. At Capharnaum, the day after the multiplication of the loaves, He taught the crowd that they would have to eat His flesh and drink His blood, under pain of not having life. If He had explained to them that it would be bread and wine transformed internally, by a miracle, into His flesh and blood, doubtless they would have accepted His word without any more difficulty than we do. However, He demanded a blind faith in His doctrine. Rather than give an explanation, He permitted thousands of listeners, who had come to Him enthusiastically, to leave Him, discouraged by His requirements.

The consequence of this complete donation of oneself is a complete, universal, and constant renunciation, both internal and external. "If anyone wishes to come after me, let him deny himself, and take up his cross daily, and follow me" (Lk 9:23). St. Luke, reporting this word of the Master, remarks that He made it to everybody. For those who listened to Jesus, His word was far more terrifying than for us. By "cross" we mean any trouble. The word has lost almost all of its real meaning from its frequent usage since Christ's death on the cross. How did His listeners understand Him? They had many an occasion to meet a malefactor carrying his cross, followed by Roman soldiers. At the place of torture, he would be fixed to it to suffer an excruciating agony which sometimes lasted for days.

A disciple of Christ, then, has to be *ready for every sacrifice,* even the most difficult. That means, for the sacrifice of *whatever might be an obstacle,* however dear it might be. "If thy hand or thy foot is an occasion of sin to thee, cut it off and cast it from thee! It is better for thee to enter life maimed or lame, than, having two hands or two feet, to be cast into the everlasting fire" (Mt 18:8–9).

THE SACRIFICE OF FAMILY TIES. "I have come to set a man at variance with his father, and a daughter with her mother, and a daughter-in-law with her mother-in-law; and a man's enemies will be those of his own household. He who loves father or mother more than me is not worthy of me; and he who loves son or daughter more than me is not worthy of me" (Mt 10:35–37).

Love for family ought not to delay the sacrifice of oneself for Jesus. "And he said to another, 'Follow me.' But he said,

'Lord, let me first go and bury my father.' But Jesus said to him, 'Leave the dead to bury their dead, but do thou go and proclaim the kingdom of God.' And another said, 'I will follow thee, Lord; but let me first bid farewell to those at home.' Jesus said to him, 'No one, having put his hand to the plow and looking back, is fit for the kingdom of God'" (Lk 9:59–62).

SACRIFICE IN PERSECUTIONS. "No disciple is above his teacher, nor is the servant above his master. It is enough for the disciple to be like his teacher, and for the servant to be like his master . . . for they will deliver you up to councils, and scourge you in their synagogues, and you will be brought before governors and kings for my sake, for a witness to them and to the Gentiles" (Mt 10:24–25; 17–18).

AT THE COST OF ONE'S LIFE. "For he who would save his life will lose it; but he who loses his life for my sake will save it" (Lk 9:24). "And brother will hand over brother to death, and the father his child; children will rise up against parents, and put them to death. And you will be hated by all for my name's sake; but he who has persevered to the end will be saved. . . . And do not be afraid of those who kill the body but cannot kill the soul. But rather be afraid of him who is able to destroy both soul and body in hell. . . . Everyone who acknowledges me before men, I will also acknowledge him before my Father in heaven. But whoever disowns me before men, I in turn will disown him before my Father in heaven" (Mt 10:21–33).

Nature shudders at times when confronted with the terrible renunciations which the Master demands of His disciples, and almost withdraws in dismay. Jesus clearly expects us to carry our cross. He carried His before us, a cross a thousand times heavier than ours. He was innocent, while we merit chastisement for our sins. It was for love of us that He carried His. Besides, the Christian who, up to this point has sincerely contemplated the infinite marvels of Christ's soul, will understand, or at least begin to understand, that the mystery of the cross is pre-eminently a mystery of love; he has caught a glimpse of the truth that, in the service of the Master, to suffer is to love.

Jesus wished to render this law of complete self-donation and total renunciation not only less appalling to us, but even more attractive, by another approach — that of Mary. He presented that law, first of all, to His Mother. Like Him, she obeyed that law, in all its rigor, from her Immaculate Conception to her blessed death, and at the cost of what sacrifices! (See Chapter 20.)

Mary helps us carry our daily cross, first by her example. She, too, had to suffer, and more than any one of us will ever have to suffer. She, too, was innocent. She, too, suffered in our stead, to save us from hell. She helps us carry our cross, by making us understand that the mystery of the cross is a mystery of love, showing us that she is happy to suffer out of love, for Jesus and for us. She helps us, also, with the grace of courage and strength, which, as Mediatrix of all Graces, she obtains for us. She even invented another means to ease that law of total donation, namely, total consecration to herself which she suggests to her most faithful children, because we do not give ourselves totally and without reserve to her except in order to belong totally and without reserve to Jesus. And so, what frightens nature, the love of Mary lightens with courage and often even with joy.

Chapter 43

RENOUNCING THE WORLD

There is another renunciation which Jesus demands of His disciples, renouncing a reality which they all encounter, and which is diametrically opposed to the doctrine and spirit of Christ, namely, the world.

The term *world* on the lips of Jesus has several meanings. Sometimes it signifies all mankind: "You are the light of the world" (Mt 5:14). Sometimes, the earth: "since the foundation of the world" (Mt 13:35). Sometimes it means the goods of this world: "What does it profit a man if he gain the whole world, but suffer the loss of his own soul?" (Mt 16:26.) Ordinarily, especially in St. John, it means the men whose view of life and whose conduct Jesus anathematizes, because they are directly opposed to His teachings, His principles, and His entire mission on earth.

They are the men who, really and generally without thinking of it, are the disciples of the devil, "the prince of this world" (Jn 14:30; 16:11). They hate Christ and His followers, because the latter are not of the world from which Christ called them (cf. Jn 15:18-19). They are incapable of receiving the Spirit of Truth, whom they do not see, and whom they do not know (cf. Jn 14:17). They persecute the faithful disciples and lead the weak into sin. "Woe to the world because of scandals" (Mt 18:7). They take the broad way that leads to destruction, and many there are who enter that way (cf. Mt 7:13).

Briefly, they are the men for whom the present life is the only one that counts, and is their last end, if not in theory, at least in practice. On the contrary, for the followers of Christ, the present life is only a means toward the true life, a very short preparation for an eternal and infinitely happy life.

According to these different conceptions of life, that of Christ and that of the world, everything here below takes an opposite signification. For the followers of Christ, blessed are the poor, the hungry, those who weep, the persecuted, those who refrain from vengeance, the insulted, the tortured, the calumniated for the sake of Christ. On the contrary, woe to the rich, to the satiated, to pleasure-seekers, and to those well-spoken of and flattered (cf. Mt 5:3–12; Lk 6:20–26). To the world, the eight beatitudes are eight follies, and the four woes are four beatitudes.

Generally the maxims of the world are true in one sense and false in another. That is precisely their danger. Completely false, they would easily be rejected. True in one sense, they risk being accepted so much the more readily by those followers of Christ who are inclined to compromise between what seems common sense and the mind of Christ.

Thus: "Life consists of compromises." True, in earthly interests; false, for Christ's teachings. "Youth must have its fun." Yes, for innocent games and sports; no, for amusements condemned by Christian morality. "We must not be so narrow, or so scrupulous." Correct, if there is question of real narrow-mindedness or scruples; wrong, if those words simply belittle loyalty to Christ's law.

One maxim, especially, is universally current, on whose authority even presumed fervent Catholics seriously and sometimes shockingly pervert the teachings of our Lord. They accept immodest fashions, sharp practice in business, exploitation of the defenseless, questionable associations, and similar conduct under the convenient catchword, "Everybody's doing it," or "You have to keep up with the rest of the world."

In His sermon on the Mount, Jesus said: "Enter by the narrow gate. For wide is the gate and broad is the way that leads to destruction, and many there are who enter that way. How narrow the gate and close the way that leads to life! And few there are who find it" (Mt 7:13). And again, "No man can

serve two masters" (Mt 6:24). And again, "He who is not with
me is against me, and he who does not gather with me scatters" (Mt 12:30).

St. Paul, so full of the spirit of the Master, wrote to the
Corinthians: "Do not bear the yoke with unbelievers. For what
has justice in common with iniquity? Or what fellowship has
light with darkness? What harmony is there between Christ
and Belial?" (2 Cor 6:14–15.) But where in the four Gospels
or in which of the fourteen Epistles of St. Paul is it said, "Do
as everybody does"?

After all, the spirit of the world is the negation of all that
Christ stands for in this world, the destruction of His entire
work, and the loss of all the souls for whom He shed His blood.
That accounts for His fierce opposition to this spirit of the
world. His love for us even demands that of Him.

The disciples' love for Christ demands of them, of course, an
attitude full of charity for the men infected with this spirit, but
an attitude as intransigent as that of their Master against the
spirit itself. Whoever is not for Him is against Him!

It must be admitted that the teaching of Christ about the
world is not well understood. The maxims of the world are so
universally repeated that they are accepted as first principles,
undisputed and indisputable as if they were self-evident.

To drive home to oneself the teachings of Christ about the
world and to live according to them, it is necessary to contemplate Christ enamored of humility, poverty, self-forgetfulness, and suffering, for love of us.

United in this contemplation with Mary — herself so enamored
with this humility, with this poverty, with this confidence in God,
all of which she chants in her *Magnificat*, and in which she sees
the cause of her greatness and happiness — we will understand
better and love more sincerely those virtues unknown to the
world, which render us so similar and so dear to our Elder
Brother and our Mother.

Chapter 44

MY YOKE IS SWEET

These demands of Christ on His disciples are, in brief, a reversal of all human values, a direct challenge to what is generally called "common sense." They change all the points of view from which the Jews of His time and men of all times judge the value of things. The definition which Father Chaminade gave of a true religious might be applied to the true Christian: "He is a man from another world." To live according to the teachings of Jesus, we have to be fools, foolish with the folly of the cross.

And still, one day the Master dared to say to those around Him: "Come to me, all you who labor and are burdened, and I will give you rest. Take my yoke upon you, and learn from me, for I am meek and humble of heart; and you will find rest for your souls. For my yoke is easy, and my burden light" (Mt 11:28–30).

That Jesus was meek and humble of heart has been affirmed by those who drew near to Him on every occasion. But was His yoke easy and His burden light? Did not the Master really come to proclaim a paradox? He compels us to accept, in everyday life, the blessedness of the poor, the hungry, the hated, persecuted, and proscribed; the misfortune of the rich, the renowned, the powerful, and pleasure-seekers; the wisdom of avoiding grave sin at the cost of such exorbitant sacrifices as of an eye, a hand, or a foot; scorn, calumny, public condemnation, and death for the sake of religion; citation before a court by one's parents, children, brothers, and sisters; hatred from all sides. Is that an easy yoke and a light burden?

Yes, for the disciple who believes in Him and loves Him.

First of all, to the transient pleasures of life which, even for those called the "upper four hundred," consist more of vexations, deceptions, dissatisfactions, jealousies, fits of anger, and hatreds than of sincere, profound, and completely satisfying joys, we are asked to prefer another life. This is an eternal life, whose joys absolutely satisfy the soul, and are beyond human imagination, a real participation in the infinite beatitude of God Himself. A believer has to fear the evidence itself, not those who kill the body, but Him who can cast body and soul into hell; "for what does it profit a man, if he gain the whole world, but suffer the loss of his own soul? Or what will a man give in exchange for his soul?" (Mt 16:26.)

But even the earthly life of a true believer is far preferable to that of a sinner. He enjoys to the full a peace which, according to St. Paul, "surpasses all understanding." Christ Himself said: "Peace I leave with you, my peace I give to you; not as the world gives do I give to you" (Jn 14:27). That is, Christ's peace is unknown to the sinner.

Even in his trials, the believer knows all kinds of joy. He knows the joy of always doing the will of God, his Father in heaven.

He knows the joy of giving, of giving himself without reserve, to God and his neighbor. The world is preoccupied with always amassing more; the believer, with always giving more. And Jesus said, "It is more blessed to give than to receive" (Acts 20:35).

He knows the joy of self-possession. The worldly man does not possess himself; he is possessed — possessed by his riches, his ambition, his passions, his worries, his fears, and his desires. He is a slave, and he is as unhappy as a slave. The believer is in full possession of himself, because he possesses himself in God. Now, self-possession is a wealth incomparably sweeter than the possession of all the goods of this earth.

He knows the joy of causing joy, of causing joy to Jesus, Mary, and his neighbor. That joy is tremendously satisfying, besides being a support in all his trials.

There is joy in his struggles, even in his tribulations. Privations, fatigues, blows, and wounds mean nothing to a victorious soldier. The soldier of Christ is always certain of victory. Christ promised it: "I say to you, my friends: Do not be afraid of those who kill the body, and after that have nothing more that they can do. . . . Are not five sparrows sold for two farthings? And yet not one of them is forgotten before God. Yes, the very hairs of your head are all numbered. Therefore do not be afraid, you are of more value than many sparrows" (Lk 12:4–7). "You shall weep and lament, but the world shall rejoice; and you shall be sorrowful, but your sorrow shall be turned into joy. A woman about to give birth has sorrow, because her hour has come. But when she has brought forth the child, she no longer remembers the anguish for her joy that a man is born into the world. And you therefore have sorrow now; but I will see you again, and your heart shall rejoice, and your joy no one shall take from you. . . . In the world you will have affliction. But take courage, I have overcome the world" (Jn 16:20–22, 33).

But this joy can only fill him who gives himself without reserve. He who tries to compromise with the world will always be unhappy. To him who gives himself entirely to Christ, Christ gives Himself entirely.

Habitual union with Mary is particularly suited to lighten the yoke of Christ and ease its burden, because in that union the necessary dispositions for carrying the yoke of the Lord are acquired most naturally. At Mary's side simplicity, humility, purity, and detachment come without effort. In habitual touch with her, without knowing how, we begin to think, to feel, to will, and to act like her. And these dispositions create a climate of peace in the soul, as well as contentment and expansion, which render any effort ten times easier.

Loving her, we naturally love those whom she loves; above all her Son, but also her other children who surround us. And the sacrifices, which our duties to Him and to them sometimes demand, are offered joyfully, because we love Jesus and our neigh-

bor with the heart of Mary. The donation of ourselves to Christ
and to His Brethren, made out of love for Mary, by her, and in
union with her, is more sincere, more complete, more fruitful,
and also much easier. Even in great sacrifices that can be demanded, the Marian soul more readily senses how easy the yoke
of Christ is, and how light His burden.

Chapter 45

VARIETY OF ATTITUDES AMONG THE AUDITORS OF JESUS

Jesus preached to everybody, but not everybody received His words in the same dispositions. He himself sketched those diverse attitudes in His parable of the Sower (cf. Mt 13:19–23).

THE PHARISEES. Far from accepting the teachings of Jesus, they were too preoccupied to contradict Him; and except for one or the other, like Nicodemus and Joseph of Arimathea, they always became more callous in their evil dispositions. Jesus said of them: "If I had not come and spoken to them, they would have no sin. But now they have no excuse for their sin" (Jn 15:22).

THE INDIFFERENT. They were too engrossed in worldly affairs to become interested in His teachings. If they happened to meet Jesus, they saw in Him only an enthusiast or a fool, and made sport of Him. Among these were Herod and his court, some Sadducees, the crowd in the house of Jairus, whose daughter had just died, and many of the rich and idle.

THE ENTHUSIASTIC CROWDS. In general, the crowds listened to Jesus. His forcefulness, His kindness, graciousness, and miracles won them. Their reactions, however, were varied.

ADMIRATION. They admired His teaching. St. Matthew remarks at the end of the Sermon on the Mount: "The crowds were astonished at his teaching; for he was teaching them as one having authority, and not as the Scribes and Pharisees" (Mt 7:28–29). They admired His works. He had just expelled a devil from a dumb man, and the man spoke. The crowd approved: "Never has the like been seen in Israel" (Mt 9:33).

RELIGIOUS FEAR. Admiration was often mingled with a sense

of religious fear, because they concluded that God worked through Jesus. When He had proved to the Scribes, by the cure of a paralytic, His power to forgive sins, "the crowds were struck with fear, and glorified God who had given such power to men" (Mt 9:8). At sight of the tempest stilled suddenly by the word of Jesus, the disciples "being afraid, marveled, saying to one another, 'Who, then, is this, that he commands even the winds and the sea, and they obey him?' " (Lk 8:25.) That sense of mysterious fear is striking, especially in the first chapters of St. Mark (cf. Mk 4:41; 5:15, 43; 6:49, 51).

EAGERNESS. The crowds were really eager to listen to the message of Jesus to the extent of abandoning their daily occupations to hear Him. They followed Him into the desert several successive days, oblivious even to their creature comforts. Men came from afar to hear Him, even from Idumea, Transjordan, Tyre, and Sidon (Mk 3:7-8). Those crowds so thronged about Him that one day, when His cousins came to see Him, they could not reach Him (Lk 8:19); and another day, in order to have Jesus touch a paralytic, the roof above His head had to be opened (Mk 2:4).

CHANGEABLENESS. Like all crowds, those which pressed around Jesus were inconstant. At first, there was almost universal enthusiasm. Then, because of the maneuvers of the Pharisees and certain demands of Jesus, many, little by little, withdrew from Him. On His arrival at Jerusalem, after the resurrection of Lazarus, everybody cried out: "Hosanna to the Son of David! Blessed is he who comes in the name of the Lord!" And five days later, it was "Crucify Him! Crucify Him!"

Those crowds received the word with joy, but there was no depth of soul; in the moment of temptation, they allowed their loyalty to be torn from their hearts. Still, the message of Jesus was not lost upon them all forever, because after the Resurrection, many of them again believed in Him.

THE MOST INTIMATE DISCIPLES. These were the apostles and several other fervent and generous men and women.

The Apostles generally received a special call to follow Jesus.

He drew them by a mysterious attraction, each one according to his aptitudes.

The first called were John and Andrew, profoundly religious men. They heard John the Baptist, their teacher, say of Jesus, who had returned to the Jordan after His fast of forty days, "Behold the Lamb of God." Timidly the two of them followed Jesus without a word. Jesus turned and asked them, "What is it you seek?" They dared not answer frankly, "Why, you," but, "Rabbi, where dwellest thou? He said to them, 'Come and see.' They came and saw where he was staying; and they stayed with him that day," that is, to sundown. John who tells the story adds, "It was about the tenth hour," that is, four in the afternoon. They had therefore stayed with Him about two hours. What did they talk about? John does not tell us, but the two young men were won over by their experience with Him (cf. Jn 1:35–39).

Andrew then met his brother Simon, a generous, enthusiastic character, and a leader. Andrew said to him, "We have found the Messias." And he led him to Jesus. Fixing His eyes upon him, Jesus said, "Thou art Simon, the son of John; thou shalt be called Cephas (which interpreted is Peter)." That look of Jesus and the new name given, which according to the tradition of the Old Testament was the sign of a special vocation, kindled Peter with enthusiasm. Completely devoted, and ready for every sacrifice, he attached himself to the young Rabbi with his whole soul.

The next day, Jesus "found Philip," who had a rather hesitant character (cf. Jn 6:5, 7; 12:21, 22; 14:8), but was desirous of doing God's will, once he knew it. Jesus said but a word, "Follow me!" and he immediately joined the other three.

Philip had a friend, Nathaniel, of a quite different character. He was a logician but a good man. He objected to Philip, "Can anything good come out of Nazareth?" Philip did not believe in argument; he just said, "Come and see." He was certain that one look at Jesus would convince his friend as he himself had been convinced. Jesus saw him coming. He did not say, "Follow me!" but gave him two reasons for believing, His own knowledge of his honesty and a particular fact that He could not know by natural means. "Behold a true Israelite in whom there is no guile!" Nathaniel said to him, 'Whence knowest thou me?' Jesus answered and said to him, 'Before Philip called thee, when thou wast under the fig tree, I saw thee.' Nathaniel answered him and said, 'Rabbi, thou art the Son of God, thou art the King of Israel.'" That was his enthusiasm, but Jesus forthwith promised him still stronger proofs: "Amen, amen, I say to you, you shall see heaven opened, and the angels of God ascending and descending upon the Son of Man" (Jn 1:35-51).

Later on, after the miraculous catch of fish, when there was question of Peter, Andrew, James, and John following the Master, not only from time to time, but constantly, Jesus simply said to them, "Follow me, and I will make you fishers of men." At once, they left everything, boats and nets, their goods and their families, and attached themselves to Him.

In the same way, somewhat later, from His disciples He picked twelve, "men of his own choosing," as St. Mark phrased it. When, in the synagogue of Capharnaum, after the discourse on the bread of life, many of His disciples left Him, and when Peter, in the name of the Twelve, assured Him of the loyalty of the group, Jesus emphasized the fact: "Have I not chosen you, the Twelve?" (Jn 6:71.) He was even more emphatic in the discourse after the Last Supper: "You have not chosen me, but I have chosen you" (Jn 15:16).

And still, these intimate disciples were also slow in understanding. It would not be until after His Ascension, when the Master would no longer be among them, that the Holy Spirit would give them the perception of what He meant by the kingdom of God. Jesus had to have infinite patience not to be irritated by their earthly ideas, their petty vanities, jealousies, and ambitions.

Nevertheless they were all, except Judas, simple, honest, generous men, devoted, body and soul, to the Master. They followed Him blindly. If they were weaker than they thought, they were, at least, sincere in their devotion to His cause. They received the word of God in fertile ground, and in God's good hour they would bring forth fruit, some sixtyfold, others a hundredfold — the thirtyfold was for the simple faithful.

LESSONS WHICH APOSTOLIC SOULS MAY DRAW FROM THIS DIVERSITY OF ATTITUDES AMONG THE AUDITORS OF JESUS.

1. Even when our Lord preached, certain listeners did not believe, and among the believers, His word was not equally efficacious. The sanctification of a man is a personal problem which depends more upon his intimate dispositions than upon external circumstances.

2. You cannot use pure enthusiasm, sincere though it be, as a foundation for supernatural ideals. As long as the latter do not rest on solid convictions and do not lead to a change of life, they run the risk of remaining without fruit.

3. A complete change of disposition, even in well-disposed persons, takes time. Our Lord Himself, after years of inspiring teaching which was confirmed by miracles, was far from revolutionizing the dispositions of men even as sincere and generous as the Apostles. However, they finished by becoming great saints.

4. We must remember that, if, despite misunderstandings and opposition, Jesus succeeded, it was because, to preaching and miracles, He added uninterrupted prayer and the price of His Passion.

God wishes the salvation of all men. Christ shed His blood for all. Mary prayed, suffered, and sacrificed her Son for all her other children. This means, not only for those who know their Savior at the present moment or who will know Him when the Gospel is preached to every creature, but also for those millions who do not know Him now, and for the billions who will never know Him to the end of time. If God wished their salvation, He made it possible. We can, therefore, contribute to their salvation not only by direct action but by prayer and suffering united to those of Jesus and Mary.

Conclusion

To the Apostles, who had questioned Him about the meaning

of the parable of the sower, Jesus explained that "the seed is the word of God."

The word of God is the varied teaching of the Master to His followers. But the word of God is also, and pre-eminently, the Word of God, the Son of God.

The seed falls on different kinds of ground and produces fruit correspondingly. There is no doubt that we must consider the readers of this book, the last page of which we have reached, as the "good ground" of Jesus, because they have produced fruit in abundance.

The abundance, however, is not the same for every kind of good ground. One kind of ground produces thirtyfold, another sixty, and a third a hundredfold. The last kind produces as much as the other two put together, and three times as much as the first. In the interest of the salvation of the greatest number of souls, our ground must not only be fertile, but fertile to the maximum degree.

We have sketched the conditions necessary for a Christian truly to understand the soul of Christ and to reproduce His dispositions which make "good ground" of a Christian. Those conditions are: generosity or love that gives itself, recollection, humility, and simplicity, in addition to union with Mary. If this union is intimate, it includes the three other conditions in a high degree, and disposes the soul to be good ground and to yield the hundredfold.

The soul constantly united with Mary lives more and more the same life that she lives; it shares in her love, her recollection, her humility, and her simplicity. Through Mary the soul will live the perfect life of Jesus. It will then discover by personal experience the truth of the claims of St. Pius X: "There is no surer or easier way than Mary by which men can reach Jesus Christ, to obtain through Jesus Christ that perfect adoption of sons which makes them holy and without stain in the eyes of God."